Turning Wood with Carbide Tools

Techniques and Projects for Every Skill Level

Turning Wood with Carbide Tools

Techniques and Projects for Every Skill Level

John English

LINDEN PUBLISHING

Fresno

Turning Wood with Carbide Tools: Techniques and Projects for Every Skill Level
by John English

©John English

Cover design: James Goold / Design and Layout: Maura J. Zimmer / Photography by John English
ISBN: 978-1-61035-054-9
Printed in China
135798642

Linden Publishing titles may be purchased in quantity at special discounts for educational,
business, or promotional use. To inquire about discount pricing, please refer to the contact information
below. For permission to use any portion of this book for academic purposes, please contact the
Copyright Clearance Center at www.copyright.com

Library of Congress Cataloging-in-Publication Data

English, John.

Turning wood with carbide tools : techniques and projects for every skill level / John English.

p. cm.

Includes index.

Summary: "Everything a woodturner needs to know about using and implementing the exciting new technology of replaceable carbide cutting tips is included in this guide. Woodturning tools have taken a quantum leap since the recent introduction of these tips that have greatly simplified the task of turning in dry stock. Carbide-tipped woodturning tools are safer, faster, easier, and more efficient than traditional tools that require grinding the end of a piece of fluted steel to one of dozens of subjective profiles. The technology of the carbide cutters is fully explained, as are the various shafts and the function of the handle designs, providing insight into how and why these cutters act as they do, and why they are shaped as they are. Removing the intimidating aspects of turning, the guide explains the elimination of sharpening, addresses the issues of chatter and fatigue, and advises on maintenance, techniques, and usage. A number of projects are included--such as a candlestick, spinning tops, and a basic bowl--that can be completed right away by novice turners, rather than waiting for years to gain enough experience to do the same job with traditional tools"-- Provided by publisher.

ISBN 978-1-61035-054-9 (pbk.)

1. Turning (Lathe work) 2. Carbide cutting tools. I. Title.

TT201.E55 2012

684'.083--dc23

2012010099

*The Woodworker's
Library*®

Linden Publishing, Inc.
2006 S. Mary
Fresno, CA 93721
www.lindenpub.com

Acknowledgments

The author and the publisher would like to thank everyone who helped create this work, including but not limited to Tom Walz of Carbide Processors, Inc.; Bill McKnight of CarbideDepot.com; Eddie Castelin; Craig Jackson of Easy Wood Tools; Mike Hunter of Hunter Tool Company; Jack McDaniel of Jewelwood Studios/Eliminator; Mark Morrison of Carbide Wood Turning Tools; Peter Cribari of Wood-of-1-Kind; Joe Rollings of Unique Tool; Mike Jackofsky of Hollow-Pro Tools; and woodturning teacher Sam Angelo from Worland, Wyoming.

Special thanks to Denny Zimmerman, Ken Froelich, Larry Kellogg, Dr. Max Durgin and Greg Raisanen for their help, and friendship.

Table of Contents

Introduction..1

Chapter 1: **The Nature of Carbide Insert Cutters**..5
Sidebar: Classification of 'C' grades of tungsten carbide..7

Chapter 2: **A Survey of Available Tools**..15
Sidebar: Making Your Own Tools & Handles..30

Chapter 3: **Technique: How to Use Carbide Tools**..33

Chapter 4: **Turning Between Centers**..43
Project 1: A Hickory Candlestick..43

Chapter 5: **Basic Bowl Turning with Flat Cutters**..51
Project 2: A Mixed Species Bowl..51
Project 3: A Lidded Bowl..56

Chapter 6: **Basic Bowl Turning with Concave Cutters**..63
Project 4: Red Oak Undercut Pot..63

Chapter 7: **Simple Hollow Vessels**..69
Project 5: Cross-grain Oak Vase..69
Project 6: Long-grain Ash Vase..74

Chapter 8: **Compound Hollow Vessels**..85
Project 7: Mahogany and Maple Urn..85

Chapter 9: **Finials**..95
Project 8: A Maple Finial..97

Chapter 10: **The Turning Workshop: Lumber, Lathes, Dust and Safety**..105

Sources..122

Index..126

Introduction

"I've often thought how nice it is to enjoy a pursuit like woodturning in which there are no firm do's and don'ts. To be sure, we have to observe basic safety measures, learn how to ride the bevel, keep a sharp edge, and other basics. But beyond the fundamentals, the field is open to anything you want to try—so long as you get the result you want." That's a quote from American Association of Woodturners (AAW) board member Stan Wellborn, in an e-mail that he sent to the membership in August 2011.

Stan is right on the money when he speaks of turning as something with no rules beyond safety, and lots of innovation. Those two qualities have allowed his wonderful organization to grow to more than 14,000 members around the globe. The AAW has played a huge part in the evolution of turning from a quiet art into one of the most popular pastimes in America.

It's not just the numbers that are growing: it's also the technology. One sign of how quickly things are evolving is that the advent of carbide insert cutters has obviated two of the three basics that Stan mentions. These relatively new tools eliminate both the need to keep a sharp edge, and the necessity to master the tricky skill of "riding a bevel". That's when one holds a gouge at a specific angle so that it slices through wood fibers most efficiently. It takes a lot of practice to master.

This new technology of replaceable carbide inserts has greatly simplified turning, especially in dry stock, and has completely done away with the need to learn how to sharpen. New and intermediate skills turners are overwhelmingly impressed

The author is a member of AAW, which has more than 14,000 members worldwide.

with carbide, and are purchasing the tools at an impressive rate. Unfortunately, many highly skilled turners are a bit slower to accept them, perhaps because carbide circumvents a large portion of the hard-won traditional skills they have learned. It dramatically simplifies most aspects of the turning process, both between centers and faceplate work, and eliminates much of the traditional learning curve. There is also a perception that carbide doesn't work as well in green wood, and the top turners almost all work in that medium as they create hollow vessels. New turners work primarily in dry stock and always have, because they concentrate

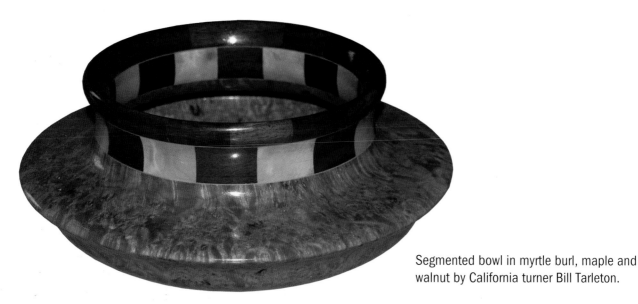

Segmented bowl in myrtle burl, maple and walnut by California turner Bill Tarleton.

on simple bowls and projects between centers, rather than deep vessels. They also purchase kiln dried wood conveniently at the lumberyard, rather than scouring the ditches with a chainsaw in hand. And even when they graduate from making simple bowls, most hobbyists tend to stay with dry stock and often become segmented turners.

Here, then, are some of the reasons for the soaring popularity of the new carbide-insert turning tools:

1. They completely eliminate sharpening.

Traditional turning tools constantly need to be sharpened and this presents a number of problems, especially for new turners. Each time a tool is introduced to the grinder, the profile changes slightly (even when using the most advanced jigs). The tool also gets shorter. Many tools, especially

It takes practice to learn how to create a fingernail grind on a fluted bowl gouge.

bowl gouges, require a special grind such as a fingernail that can take a long time to learn. The turner must become part metalworker, especially when masters in the field advocate long sweeps or negative angles or other modifications that are both confusing and challenging. A new turner using traditional tools must learn about grinding wheel composition, hardness, grit, speeds and quenching. He or she must also learn a fair amount of geometry to conquer the compound profiles that must be created. Sharpening is so challenging that an informal survey of lathe students at the Black Hills School of Woodworking revealed that 81% of new turners thought it was the single greatest impediment to their advancement

Beyond the complexity, time is an issue. One of the new carbide cutters outlasts a high-speed steel (HSS) edge somewhere in the neighborhood of 120 times, according to several of the tool manufacturers. If a trip to the grinder takes ten minutes, that's about twenty hours that can be spent turning instead of sharpening during the life of a single carbide insert! It's easy to see the attraction of not having to sharpen.

This vessel by Anna Achtziger was made in her third session on a lathe, with carbide tools.

2. There's a remarkably short learning curve.

In an average bowl-making class, an instructor will use traditional fluted bowl gouges, usually ⅜" and ½", which he sharpens before class with a fingernail grind and a long sweep. He then spends most of the morning talking about sharpening, and the afternoon showing students how to hold the gouge for inside cuts, and then for outside cuts, and then for shearing, scraping, working with side grain and end grain. All of these require the student to think

about the angle of approach, opening and closing the face, using different parts of the grind...whew!

In classes using carbide-tipped tools, most students complete their first bowl halfway through the morning session, a couple of hours after they first turn on a lathe. There is still some technique to learn, but it's akin to the difference between teaching a teenager how to drive an automatic as opposed to a stick shift. He still needs to know the rules of the road, but he doesn't have to concentrate so hard on letting the clutch out slowly. Most new students can create complex works after just a few short classes.

Because of their cutting profiles, many of these tools are simply held parallel to the floor (there are notable exceptions, and more on this in Chapter 2). Carbide inserts cut with the front edge and also with both side edges, so they can be moved into the work and then slid along the tool rest. They cut more quickly and more cleanly than a gouge in the hands of a novice (although that's not always true for highly experienced turners), and they can be backed off for a gentle scraping that can really clean up the surface.

3. Carbide insert tools are simpler, safer and sounder.

There are essentially three carbide-tipped profiles, each available in several sizes. The cutters are round, square (or very slightly radiused), and diamond-shaped. These latter are referred to as detailers. The shafts on the better tools are heavy, square and made of stainless steel. A few hollowing tools with gooseneck shafts are available, but there are still just a few cutting profiles because that's all that is needed. This vastly simplifies the turning process for novices, and delivers quick results.

Television show host and acclaimed turner David J. Marks uses EWT's carbide insert tools.

These heavy tools with their small cutters (and the fact that the cutting edge on top of the tool rest is set dead center to the project instead of below the centerline, as with much traditional gouge work) have vastly reduced chatter and fatigue. Tools with square shafts transfer vibrations to the tool-rest more efficiently than round-shafted, lighter traditional tools that can telegraph every bump to the user's hands and arms. Used properly, they are virtually catch-free, which is a huge consideration for novices who are genuinely (and appropriately) intimidated when the tip of a gouge catches in the wood.

4. Carbide insert tools open doors for dry wood turners.

Until now, new turners working in air-dried or kiln-dried hardwoods had fewer options than their counterparts who used green blanks. Because of the learning curve, advanced projects—especially hollow vessels—were simply out of reach. Novices were stuck with basic shallow bowl forms. Carbide insert tools allow less experienced turners to tackle complex shapes, which they could not have imagined handling with traditional tools until they had hundreds of hours of practice behind them.

A hollow vessel in laminated poplar, this piece was turned by a beginner and beaded.

There are only two types of turning tools—cutters and scrapers. All of the familiar names—bowl and spindle gouges, skews, parting tools—fall into these two categories. Despite that, turning has always been a complex process because one needed to know when to use each. Grain direction was paramount, and determined which of several tools in the arsenal would be most appropriate. Now, a beginning or intermediate turner needs just a round carbide cutter, a square one, and a detailer. These new tools are a hybrid: the cutting power of a gouge and the ease of a scraper.

CHAPTER 1

The Nature of Carbide Insert Cutters

"Carbide" is a misnomer.

The material used to make inserts for lathe turning tools is actually tungsten carbide, an inorganic chemical compound containing both tungsten and carbon atoms in a cobalt binder. The woodworking industry has referred to it as simply "carbide" for so long that we tend to forget about the tungsten. The newest generation of this material uses smaller grain sizes and has been given the nickname "nano-carbide". (Nano literally means one billionth, and is used colloquially to describe very small particles.) There are also a few ceramic and metal/ceramic inserts available, but most of the manufacturers use tungsten carbide.

People have been familiar with carbon since our ancestors made charcoal in their fires to create petroglyphs. High school chemistry students know that its chemical symbol is C and its atomic number is 6. They also know that carbon is not a metal, but

TOM LOOMIS, DAKOTA MATRIX MINERALS

Tungsten is only found in compound with other elements, as here with iron and manganese.

it combines easily with several metals. Tungsten (W) is a metal. In nature, it is only found in a compound with another element. The photograph here (above) is of "wolframite" which, according to geological engineer Tom Loomis of Dakota Matrix Minerals in Rapid City, South Dakota, is a tungstate of iron and manganese.

Combined with carbide, tungsten is familiar to woodworkers on router bits and saw blades.

Carbide cutters are extremely hard, but brittle. These contacted the jaws of a chuck.

Tungsten has been isolated and used in industry since the late 1700s, and as a compound it is familiar to woodworkers in the form of saw-blade tips, router bit inserts and other woodshop cutters (above). One reason it has been so useful is that it has an extremely high tolerance for heat. It's also very dense (about the same as gold), and in its pure form it is quite ductile (workable).

When these two elements are combined at about 2400°F (1300°C), they form tungsten carbide (WC), a metallic compound that is several times stronger and denser than steel. It's also harder and more brittle than steel, and can only be sharpened with a handful of abrasives, most notably diamond. Tungsten carbide will remain in bond up to an amazing 5200°F. So, unlike high-speed steel, heat build-up on a carbide insert while turning wood is not an issue.

Tungsten carbide is so durable that it is routinely used to cut aluminum and other soft metals, and some grades are actually capable of cutting right through the tool steel of our traditional gouges and scrapers. Because of its hardness, it is somewhat brittle and its edge can shatter from the shock of,

for example, accidentally hitting the revolving metal jaws of a chuck (above). But in general, a knot is no match for the new cutters. Tungsten carbide is also quite resistant to corrosion, so turners in green wood don't need to worry about rust.

One healthy advantage to carbide insert cutters is that, because they are not sharpened, there is no need to release fine metal particles from the sharpening process into the woodshop's air.

Grades of Tungsten Carbide

The simplest way to think about carbide grades is that the low numbers are most resistant to shock and the high numbers are most resistant to wear. There's a trade-off here. C1 is not very brittle and is quite resistant to shock and impact in materials such as stone, brick and concrete. But it's not the hardest compound and loses its edge more quickly than other grades. Tungsten carbides in the C5 and above region hold an edge for a very long time unless they meet something hard that shocks them. Impacts will shatter their edges more readily than happens with the low grades. In wood, higher grades (C3 and C4) deliver a sharper cut for a longer time.

"Carbide" is actually tungsten carbide grains cemented together with a binder such as cobalt.

Most carbide insert manufacturers are reluctant to tell the public what grade they are using. One might think that they just don't want to share this information with the competition, but Tom Walz, the president of Carbide Processors, Inc. in Tacoma, Washington, says things aren't quite that simple.

"Tungsten carbide is actually tungsten carbide grains cemented together with a binder such as cobalt (above)," Tom said. "You can do a lot of different things with tungsten carbide by changing the grain size and the amount of cobalt in it. You can also add small amounts of other material to create special grades of tungsten carbide, much as adding a little chrome or nickel to steel makes stainless steel.

"During World War II the United States Army and Buick came up with the 'C' classification system for tungsten carbide. There are nineteen C grades overall, with grades C-1 to C-4 rated as general grades for cast iron, non-ferrous and non-metallic materials. These are the typical woodworking grades and are generally used thus: C-1 for roughing, C-2 for general purpose, C-3 for finishing and C-4 for precision.

Classification of 'C' Grades of Tungsten Carbide

(C-2 to C-5 are generally the grades used in woodshop cutters.)

C-1	Roughing
C-2	General Purpose
C-3	Finishing
C-4	Precision

Steel and Steel Alloys—
these grades resist pitting and deformation

C-5	Roughing
C-6	General Purpose
C-7	Finishing
C-8	Precision

Wear Surface

C-9	No shock
C-10	Light shock
C-11	Heavy shock

Impact

C-12	Light
C-13	Medium
C-14	Heavy

Miscellaneous

C-15	Light cut, hot flash weld removal
C-15A	Heavy cut, hot flash weld removal
C-16	Rock bits
C-17	Cold header dies
C-18	Wear at elevated temperatures and/or resistance to chemical reactions
C-19	Radioactive shielding, counter balances and kinetic applications

Sidebar courtesy Carbide Processors, Inc.
www.carbideprocessors.com

"Historically, C-1 was a very tough, hard-to-break grade that typically had much larger grains and much more cobalt binder. C-4 was a very hard, longwearing grade with small grains and much less cobalt binder.

Tungsten carbide grades, like the size of radios, has changed a lot since the 1940s.

"In World War II a radio was a major home appliance, several feet tall, which dominated the living-room. It often had an antenna, sometimes on the roof of the house. Now ordinary radios are small enough to slip in a shirt pocket (above). Special radios are made small enough that you cannot see them. There have been similar advances in tungsten carbide. Just as a radio still performs the same function, a C-1 grade is still tough and the C-4 grade is still longwearing. The difference is that today's C-4 is much, much tougher than the old C-1 ever was. And the new C-1 is much longer wearing than the old C-4 was.

"Just as the radio of World War II has evolved into television, computers and cell phones, so carbide grades have evolved into things such as nail cutter grades, Super C multi-grades, Cermet and Cermet 2 grades, and a host of other special grades.

"Some manufacturers still use the designation C-4 for their carbide saw tips when it should be more like 'Super Multi-grade C1.5 to C4.5++' because the grade they are calling C-4 is very tough and very long wearing, with other special properties such as corrosion resistance and increased lubricity to make it easier for the tip to slide through the material being cut. However, the term C-4 is much more familiar. In addition, it would take up most of the package to list all the benefits of modern grades compared to the traditional C-4 grade."

In his book *Building Superior Brazed Tools* (cafepress.com, #030-224146572) (right), Tom Walz begins a discussion on carbide grades by saying that "there is no comprehensive comparison of tungsten carbide between and among tungsten carbide suppliers. A big part of

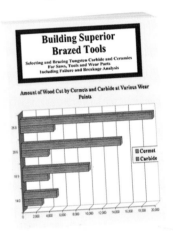

To understand tungsten carbide, visit Tom Walz at carbideprocessors.com, or read his books.

the problem is the huge number of suppliers, grades and trade names. There are at least 5,000 different grades of tungsten carbide sold under more than 1,500 different trade names by more than 1,500 different companies. There is no true standard. The US 'C' designation, the ISO designation and other designations are not necessarily relevant. Tungsten carbide from two different manufacturers may have an identical designation but vary widely in almost every imaginable way, including performance."

So, when a carbide insert lathe tool manufacturer decides not to reveal what grade of tungsten carbide is being used in his or her inserts, it may be because it's simply beyond description.

All of the projects shown here were turned by the author, using just three carbide insert tools.

"The original concept was to rate tungsten carbides according to the job that they had to do," says Tom Walz. "If you had a particular job, you would specify a 'C' grade of tungsten carbide and you could buy that from anybody. This has lead to a situation where a C-7 tungsten carbide can be almost anything as long as it does C-7 style work. According to Machinery's Handbook (a classic reference work in mechanical engineering published since 1914 by Industrial Press, New York) it can range from 0 to 75% tungsten carbide, 8 to 80% titanium tungsten carbide, 0 to 10% cobalt and 0 to 15% nickel. The problem is that two C-7 tips from two manufacturers will almost certainly work very differently in two different applications.

"A common misconception is that there is a straight progression from C-1 to C-14 or wherever. A common view is that each higher grade has less cobalt in the binder and is therefore harder and more likely to break. Following this line of thought

is belief that the higher 'C' number is harder and better for wear resistance. This is like classifying automobiles by size from a moped to an eighteen-wheel semi. This is clear and handy, but unfortunately it is not true."

In general, tungsten carbide tips being made in the USA and used on woodturning lathe tools are in the C-2 to C-4 range, but as Tom explained, those numbers are quite subjective and the specifics may change from one supplier to the next, and perhaps from one batch of inserts to the next. The bottom line is that the manufacturers can worry about the grade of carbide, and turners just need to concentrate on the profiles (shapes) of the inserts, and where each is used.

Carbide Insert Shapes

The appeal of these tools, in a nutshell, is their simplicity. All of the projects shown here (above) were turned with just three profiles: a round, a

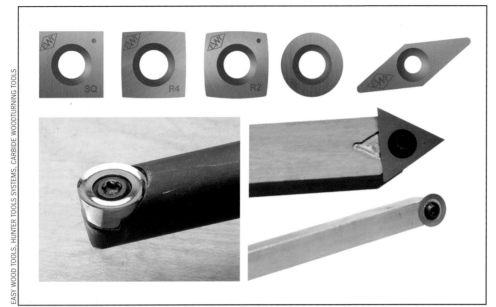

Round cutters make concave cuts, square ones shape convex cuts, and triangles do detailing.

square and a triangular cutter. The insert sizes may change, but the basic shapes stay the same. Square cutters either come as perfect squares or their edges may have a slight radius, and the angles of the triangular inserts are sometimes so acute that they are diamond-shaped.

Cutters are either flat or saucer-shaped. Manufacturers of the flat carbide insert tools recommend simply holding the handle of the tool parallel to the floor. The tool-rest height is set so that the edge of the cutter meets the widest part of the turning blank (in effect, it is centered). Then, one just pushes the tool gently into the rotating wood. There is, of course, more to it than that (see Chapter 3), but in essence these tools are a whole lot simpler to use than traditional tools performing the same tasks. The round cutters are ideal for concave cuts (as in the inside of a bowl); the square cutters work on convex (outside) curves and straight lines; and the triangular detailers do the work of parting tools, pointed gouges and even small scrapers (above).

All of the flat tools cut both on the forward thrust (with their front edge) and during lateral motion (with their sides). So, a turner can begin a curve and then sweep from side to side enlarging it, much as a traditional round-nosed scraper would be used, but at a far faster rate of removal. When Craig Jackson of Easy Wood Tools in Lexington, Kentucky first introduced his line of carbide insert tools, he was often asked whether they were 'just' scrapers. It's easy to see why turners would ask that, because the tops of his carbide inserts are flat, like scrapers.

"Tools are historically classified as scrapers," he says, "because due to their design, they can only be used that way. For example, a round-nosed high-speed steel (HSS) scraper can't be used really safely in any other way than as a scraper. All of our carbide insert tools can certainly be used in other ways, such as in shear cutting, if the user chooses to present the tool in a way other than flat and level. So our tools are not classified as scrapers. Almost any woodturning tool can be used as a scraper. A common skew can be used as a negative scraper if the user chooses to do so, simply by laying it flat on the tool rest, but that doesn't make a skew (only) a scraper.

"We promote our tools to be used just flat and level (below) because we want all of our customers to get off to a great and safe start. We find that as they build their skills, they find many other ways to use the tools (such as shear cutting), but we only recommend these more difficult cuts when the safer method of flat and level just will not achieve the cut quality needed. Why stand on one leg as you're turning, when you can stand on both?

"What classifies a tool is the way that the user chooses to present it to the wood. Different tool presentation angles or methods are sometimes needed to get the results you seek with traditional tools, but our super sharp carbide cutting edges cut so cleanly that the need to perform the complicated traditional shear cuts is almost eliminated."

Turning teachers at the Black Hills School of Woodworking have worked with lots of students

Tools with flat-topped carbide cutters such as EWT's round Finisher are held parallel to the floor.

and a wide array of experience and this has revealed a few basic truths about flat insert cutter shapes. Whether it's a straight, round or triangular-shaped insert, they all work in just about the same way. Most new turners instinctively turn to scrapers instead of gouges because they are so much easier to control and learn. They feel safer, and even though they only remove a small percentage of the material that a gouge can handle, inexperienced turners prefer to sacrifice volume for control. While gouges slice through the fibers, scrapers simply abrade them, tearing them loose.

All of the carbide insert shapes are designed to cut (shear) even though they are held and used like traditional scrapers. The confidence that this gives a new turner allows one to quickly build skills.

The Cost of Carbide Insert Tools

There is a perception among wood turners that the cost of carbide insert tools is prohibitive. The individual tools are somewhat expensive (from about $50 to $135 or so), but as one only needs a few, the cumulative cost is probably less than a comprehensive set of traditional tools (two or three spindle gouges, a couple of parting tools, three or four bowl gouges, a V-tool, some scrapers, perhaps some aftermarket handles…). And, of course, one doesn't need to invest in the endless array of sharpening machines, tools, jigs, abrasives, stones, belts, grinders and so on.

One must also consider the time investment. Tools that cut quicker and require zero trips to the sharpener deliver an unseen dividend: a whole lot more time becomes available to actually turn on the lathe.

The inserts themselves are relatively inexpensive (generally under $20). Knowing when to change cutters is an acquired skill. Because the cutters hold

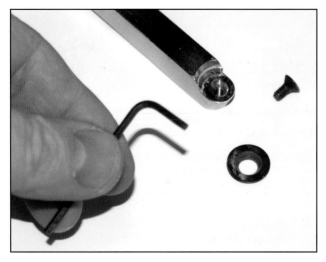

When one has to push one of these tools to get results, it's probably time to rotate the cutter.

an edge so well for so long, dullness creeps up very slowly. The first sign of it is when large amounts of material need to be removed (the inside of a bowl, for example), and it seems to be taking too much forward thrust to get the job done. If the tool needs to be pushed into the work to get results, it's probably time to rotate the cutter (above).

Another sign that a cutter is beginning to dull is when final, clean cuts aren't all that clean. Unfortunately, this isn't as simple as it sounds. The problem might be the work itself. Fast-growing or less dense species of wood often tend to be a bit "hairy". Or perhaps the tool is traveling too fast across the surface to give the cutter time to shear small fibers. To find out, simply rotate the cutter and see if things improve. If not, then it's not a dull insert that's to blame.

Choosing Tools

As with traditional lathe tools, there are lots of options when it comes to putting together a set of carbide insert tools. However, the choices are a lot simpler. At this time, there are only three basic cutter shapes (round, square and triangular), and two shaft profiles (straight and sawn neck, although

there are variants of each). So a lot of the choice comes down to the size of the cutter.

Square cutters are primarily used for convex cuts—the outside of a bowl, for example. They are wide and present more of their edge to the wood than the other shapes, so they can remove more material faster. It's a good idea to start one's collection with a large square cutter. It's also a good idea to have at least one completely square insert on hand for creating tenons to chuck work in square jaws. Many 'square' inserts have a small radius to allow them to make clean cuts without the corners digging in or leaving lines on the work.

Next, one needs a round tool. These are essential for working inside (concave) profiles, and it really helps to have both a large and a small one, to handle a number of radii. If restricted to just one, the smaller is probably more versatile. Various manufacturers offer differing round profiles. Easy Wood Tools, for example, sells inserts that are flat across the top and are very easy to control, so they have special appeal for beginners. The round inserts used by Hunter Tool Systems have a saucer shape, so they are sort of a hybrid between a flat cutter and a traditional bowl gouge. This profile definitely requires a lot more learning, but is perhaps more versatile once mastered, especially for deep hollowing. (See Chapter 2 for more details.) Ideally, a turner might own and learn how to use one of each style.

And the starter package isn't complete without a detailer (diamond-shaped cutter). This works to create square and dovetailed tenons for chucks; as a parting tool to release work; as a scoring tool to create shallow grooves for inlay and wire burning; as a skew or scraper to create small beads or coves; and even to remove most of the foot

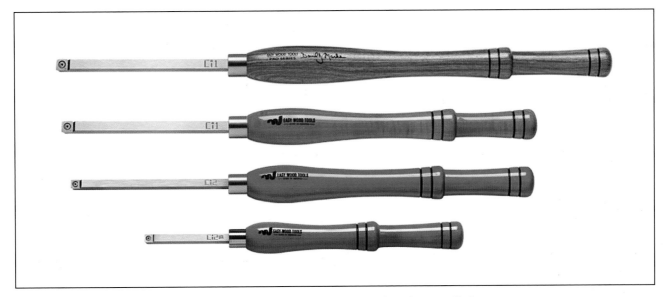

While the inserts' shapes remain the same, the size of the handle, shaft and cutter all change.

tenon when the mouth of the work is held on a jam chuck or by expanding jaws.

Most manufacturers offer two, three and even four sizes of each tool (above). The smallest ones appeal primarily to pen turners, the medium ones work well on spindles and moderate bowls, and the large and extra large ones are primarily used for big bowls and hollow work. They are interchangeable to a degree: shaft length seems to be the biggest determining factor. For example, short tools don't reach into the work very far.

In general, cutters can't be swapped from tool to tool. For example, one can't often install a round insert in a square tool. These are precise instruments with very specific tolerances, and the engineers who design them have taken into account factors such as the stability of the insert, support under the cutting edge, and simple ergonomics (will the steel below the cutter touch the wood before the cutter does?).

There are, of course, exceptions where some manufacturers' tools will accept more than one shape or size of insert.

Shaft Shapes

The majority of carbide insert tools have a shaft that is either square or round. Some of the swan necks have a rectangular (flattened) shaft. Arguments for shapes run thus: square shafts sits solidly on the tool rest and, in the event of a catch, they tend to resist the urge to roll. Round shafts fit into small openings better and allow experienced turners to take more advantage of the cutter as a shearing tool. Perhaps what a new turner should be most concerned with is the strength of the shaft. Large, thick shafts add a lot of weight and mass to the tool, reducing vibration.

Handle Options

Most carbide insert tools are available either with or without a factory handle. Un-handled tools generally come with a ½" or ⅝" round shaft that fits into a standard aftermarket handle. The advantage to this is that one can generally select the amount (length) of the shaft that is exposed. For close work, the shaft can be pushed into the handle, and for deep work it can be pulled out, making the overall tool longer. However, aftermarket handles can add considerably to the cost of a set of tools (good ones cost about the same as the tool itself),

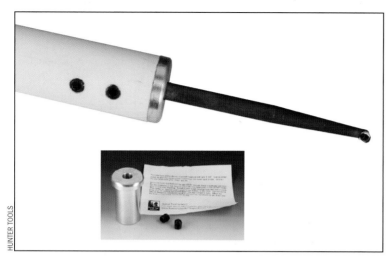

Hunter Tool Company offers kits to make one's own aluminum turning tool handles.

and there is an argument that they are not quite as solid. Here's Craig Jackson on that:

"Easy Wood Tools primarily promotes our handled tools because everything works best as a system. The balance and the push point of the Easy Grip™ handle are the best combo, in our view. We don't list un-handled tools on our Website for this reason, but they are available.

"It is our conclusion that setscrew type handles generate more vibration than a solidly fitting tool that is epoxied into a handle. We believe this is due to the much smaller point of contact, with just a couple of screw tips contacting the tool. We were developing modular handles, and in actual testing they didn't perform as well as solid fit handles. Our handles are pressed onto the tools with about 1,000

lbs. of force, and our diameter tolerances are right around +/- .001", for a proper fit."

The turning tool industry might disagree with Craig on the setscrew issue. Tool handles have been around a long time, and have a sound and reliable history. And some tools are simply not available in a handled version: they are only designed to fit into aftermarket handles. In addition, many turners prefer to make their own custom, personalized handles, for both physical and artistic reasons. Others like to use handle systems, such as Hunter Tool Company's aluminum turning tool handle sleeve kits (left). These four kits are intended to provide a low costs alternative to commercially available interchangeable tool handles. Each kit includes one sleeve (¼", ⅜", ½" or ⅝"), two setscrews and instructions.

In talking to manufacturers and experienced turners, the consensus seems to be that, if a company offers the tool with a factory-fitted handle, it is part of a design system that will most probably work best in that configuration. And just to keep things ambiguous, if a turner already owns several handles, he or she can save quite a bit on new carbide insert tools by buying them without handles.

CHAPTER 2

A Survey of Available Tools

There are a number of carbide insert lathe tool manufacturers, and perhaps the best way to illustrate the differences between their products is to visit each and describe what they offer. These companies are listed alphabetically below.

Carbide Wood Turning Tools

Based in Evansville, Indiana, this company makes tools with stainless steel shanks, carbide inserts and ash handles (or un-handled, if the customer prefers). By the fall of 2011 they had developed five lines of tools, which their Web site said "will eliminate much of the difficulty of roughing out, hollowing, and finishing wood blanks. Our tools cut down turning time from 50% to 75%, with far less strain on the turner."

Carbide Wood Turning Tools estimates that their inserts are "at least 25 to 100 times more resistant to wear than high speed steel". The range is so broad because it is difficult to compare apples to apples. Carbide tools don't replicate the shapes of traditional gouges, so any comparison needs to be tempered by that. They are not performing the same tasks in the same manner. And their tools do completely eliminate sharpening.

CRAIG JACKSON

This company, more than others, has developed a really wide selection of tools for different applications, and one of their corporate goals is to keep their product affordable. All of their tools are made in the U.S.A., and have a money-back warranty. This company only sells inserts (cutters) to people who are registered Carbide WoodTurning tool owners. Their shipping costs

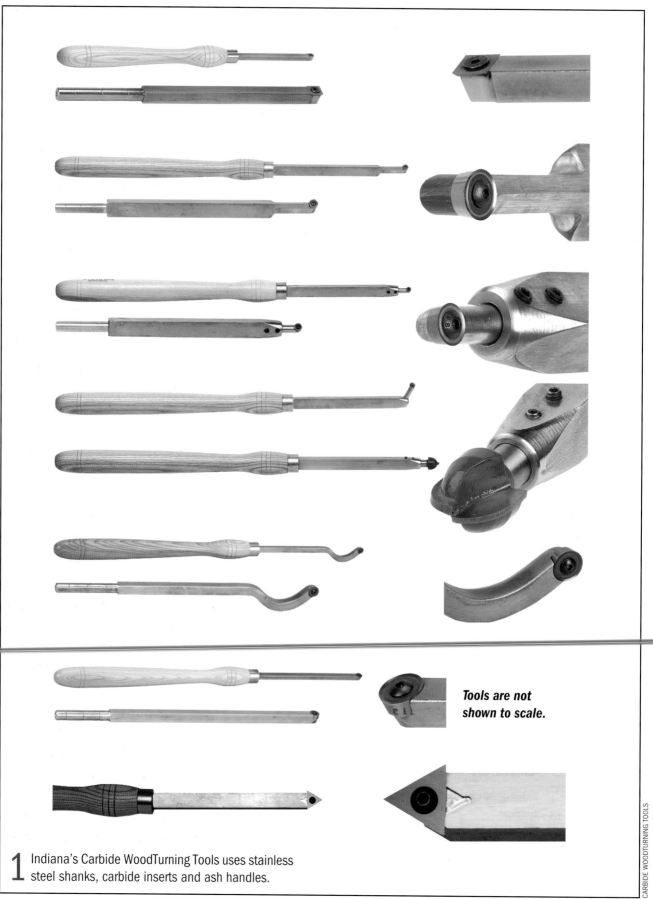

Tools are not shown to scale.

1 Indiana's Carbide WoodTurning Tools uses stainless steel shanks, carbide inserts and ash handles.

are $13.50, no matter how many tools are in the order (as of 2011).

Following is a brief summary of their five lines of tools.

The basic S Series includes five tools: a short-handled and a long-handled 10mm square cutter; a 15mm and a 17mm square; and a 16mm round.

The SS Series includes two tools, both of which can be ordered to accept any one of three different round cutters (6, 10 or 12mm). One has a straight 8½" long shaft with a 15" ash handle, and the other is a curved swan neck shaft.

The SR Series is essentially a single tool that is available in any one of five different configurations. Each insert is attached to a short round shaft that slides into a hole drilled in the end of the main tool shaft (which is square). Two set screws then hold the tool, which is preset to 0, 15, 20, 45 or 60° to the work. Each SR tool will hold either a 6mm or 10mm insert, but not both. The cutter is a saucer-shaped disc, and the company says "each of these unique angles can be used to achieve optimal results at the discretion of each individual wood turner." This adjusted angle option " is very helpful to the hollow turner where the tip cannot be seen. Since each turner prefers their own angle of offset, our tools offer 5 different angles." Worth noting is that each tool can be custom machined to any length, for the deep hollowing turner. They can also make any SR tool with a ¾" to 2½" tang, to fit in a standard arm brace handle.

There are seven tools in the next series, the SA, and what sets them apart is a one-piece, two-step shaft. The shaft emerges from the handle as either a ½" or ¾" square stainless steel bar that sits solidly on the tool rest. About three quarters of the way along its

CARBIDE WOODTURNING TOOLS

2 The Tool Brace from CWT is designed to prevent lateral and downward torque in event of a catch.

length, each bar steps down to a thinner dimension and its aspect is rotated. One of the tools turns 35° counterclockwise (using a 12mm cutter), and the other six turn 45° (using 6, 10 and 12mm cutters). The 35° version is slightly more aggressive, so it removes more wood. Three of these latter six are designated Mega, because of their robust size.

The fifth series of tools, the SRB, is designed to hold either a ¼" or a ½" carbide-tipped router bit shaft. The ¼" router bit shaft tool holds router bits up to ¾" in diameter. The ½" router bit shaft tool holds router bits from ¼" to 2" in diameter. Straight plunge bits can be used to create tenons or square cuts, while a core box bit can make quick work of the transition from the bottom of a bowl to the inside walls.

Turners using carbide insert tools to hollow deep vessels will also be interested in the Tool Brace from Carbide Wood Turning Tools (Photo 2). It is designed to prevent lateral and downward torque of the tool in event of a catch. It essentially traps carbide insert tools between the tool rest and a steel bar that is designed to stop them flying out of one's hands in the event of a problem.

Easy Wood Tools

Founded by Craig and Donna Jackson in 2008, this Kentucky-based company has a unique approach to carbide insert tooling. They have developed a complete system that includes two-step handles, stainless steel square shafts, and flat top (no cup) carbide inserts. The result is a series of well-balanced, ergonomically comfortable tools that are easy to hold, and easy to control for all skill levels.

Craig Jackson has been a metalworker (specifically a machinist and fabricator) since the mid-80s. He has also worked as an industrial design engineer and instructor, and holds a degree in machine tool technology. With that background, it's not surprising that he was frustrated by all the cutting angles, catches and sharpening methods that he encountered when he started woodturning in 2004. It didn't take him long to realize that, with his training, he could take a fresh look at traditional tools and methods. The result is a line of tools that requires no sharpening; reduces kickbacks and catches by giving the cutters a neutral cutting angle; reduces fatigue because pressure is directed into the tool rest; and eliminates riding the bevel. His standard tools come with hard maple handles and copper ferrules. TV host and noted wood turner David J. Marks endorses a line of EWT tools that includes their Pro Rougher, Pro Finisher and Pro Detailer, all with 20" bubinga handles. All EWT tools are engraved with the

3 EWT's system includes two-step handles, stainless steel square shafts, and flat carbide inserts.

carbide insert number (Ci#) on the tool bar to let users know which replacement cutter to use.

EWT tools are held flat on the rest and parallel to the floor, so that even a novice can cut left, right or straight in, and do so within minutes of picking up the tool. The line includes four tool categories—roughers, finishers, detailers and hollowers—and most come in various sizes to match a project size—mini, mid, full or pro (with 12", 14", 16" 20 handles respectively). (Photo 4).

Easy Roughers with square cutters take any one of three cutters—perfectly square, or with a 2" (R2) or 4" (R4) radius (Photo 5). This tool is designed

4 (top photo) Easy Wood Tools' rougher (top), finisher (middle) and detailer (bottom) are a complete system.

5 (bottom photo) Three variations of rougher (square, 2" radius and 4" radius) complement EWT's round cutters.

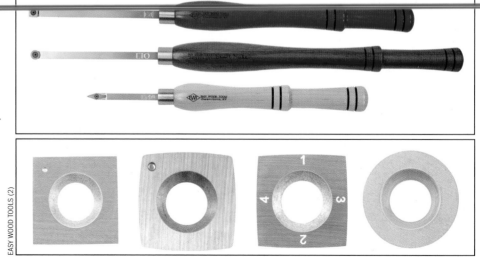

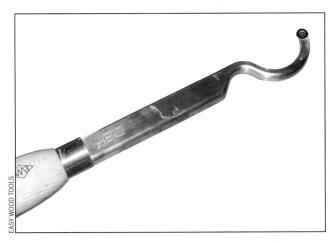

EASY WOOD TOOLS

6 EWT offers several swan neck tools with round cutters, and a straight hollower with a small insert.

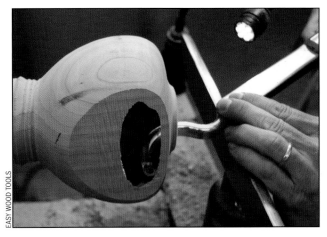

EASY WOOD TOOLS

7 The wide, heavy shaft on EWT's swan neck tools offer stability when cleaning out the shoulder.

to make the roughing cuts that get a project going. It is also used for final passes on outside curves. The slight radius eliminates lines at the edge of the cut.

Easy Finishers with round cutters are used next, to do the lighter work and inside curves. It's a good idea to have a spare cutter on hand that is dedicated to just making final passes. By switching to this cutter to clean up, and then switching back to the original cutter for the next inside curve, a turner can get a lot of mileage out of two inserts and always enjoy clean final cuts.

The hollowing tools are part of a system (Photo 6) (Photo 7), with two swan necks and a straight hollower that work together. All three have wide, flat, heavy shafts and small cutters that place them among the most stable turning tools available.

In keeping with the safe and simple theme that runs through their product line, EWT offers a full line of high quality, 8-screw, faceplates (Photo 8), and also a pair of deflector shields (Photo 9) that attach to the square shafts, and redirect waste away from the operator.

Easy Detailers, with diamond-shaped cutters, can cut decorative details, fit into tight spots, and perform detailed cuts like those required to make smaller beads and coves. All Easy Detailers use the exact same cutter.

8 (left photo) Heavy duty faceplates with eight screw holes are an example of the quality of Easy Wood Tools.

9 (right photo) A clear plastic shield from EWT safely directs shavings and chips away from the woodturner.

EASY WOOD TOOLS (2)

Harrison Specialties

Based in Elk River, Minnesota, about half an hour from Minneapolis, this company offers a complete line of carbide insert lathe tools with and without handles. Their handles are golf grips (Photo 11), and add 10" to the length of the unhandled tools. Harrison also offers a relatively inexpensive 17" foam grip handle that will accept their round-shafted or any other manufacturer's tools that have a ½" diameter tang. It's a hollow steel tube that can be filled with steel shot for added mass. The cutter shafts are locked in place with a single Allen setscrew.

Harrison's line-up includes both flat-topped and saucer-shaped cutters. They are a 16mm round hollower; a 14mm square shaper (with a square shaft that has a round tang to fit in their handle); a 14mm 90 Degree Diamond scraper (that has a square cutter set at 45 degrees); and a 55 degree diamond shaped scraper. Both the square and 90 Degree scrapers have flat-topped inserts, while the hollower has a saucer-shaped insert. The 55-degree scraper has a diamond-shaped insert with short sidewalls (Photo 12). Square, flat cutters are also available with 4" and 6" radii (slight curves) for blended cuts.

Kerry Harrison has created a number of instructional/demo videos that are posted on the Harrison Specialties Web site. The company also has a very interesting budget laser system for hollowing, and they sell vacuum chucks.

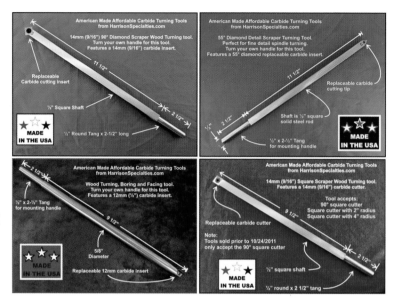

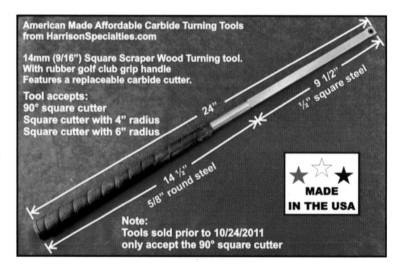

10 The line-up from Harrison Specialties includes both flat-topped and saucer-shaped cutters.

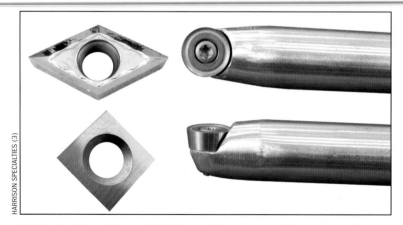

11 This 14mm square tool from Harrison has a rubber golf club handle and accomodates three cutters.

HARRISON SPECIALTIES (3)

12 Harrison offers a 55° diamond scraper and flat cutters with 4" and 6" radii for blended cuts.

Hunter Tool Systems

The product line from Hunter Tool Systems in Minneapolis, Minnesota, is focused on turners who turn hollow forms and end-grain work such as boxes, goblets, etc.

"At the heart of the system," Mike Hunter says, "is a circular structured carbide cutter that lasts up to 100 times longer than similar HSS cutters, and does not require sharpening." (Photo 13)

For people who have mastered traditional tools and want to see what carbide inserts are all about, this system offers a hybrid option that uses some of the old skills and some of the new technology. The author found that the #4 tool was aggressive when hogging, and it also sheared well on final cuts once one learned how to use it. The cutter insert is saucer-shaped with thin walls (Photo 14), and it can catch if not presented properly to the wood. The concept here is to use the plane of the tool to control the rate of cut. That is, one rotates the tool so that either more or less of the cutter is in contact with the work. Rotating means that a smaller or larger arc is doing the work. The larger the arc is (in traditional terms, the more open the face), the deeper the cut.

Hunter Tools are manufactured to high quality standards in the USA and every holder (handle) has an aluminum oxide finish to prevent rust. Both the roughing and finishing tools use the same insert. A big advantage to this system is that the saucer-shaped inserts seem to work better than flat inserts in green lumber. While that's offset to a degree by the learning curve, Hunter's swan neck tools are a joy to use because their cutters are pre-set at just the right angle for smooth cuts (Photo 15).

13 Mike Hunter's system is based on a high quality, saucer-shaped carbide cutter.

14 These four views of the same Hunter cutter also show the bevel on the bottom of the tool.

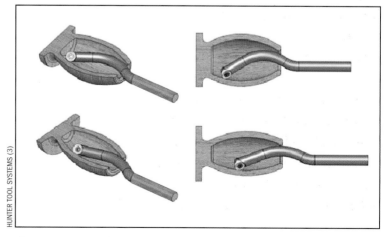

15 The cutters on Hunter's swan neck tools are pre-set at just the right angle for smooth cuts.

"The Hunter Tool Cutters work best on closed grain woods," says their Web site. "If you are working open grain woods, many wood turners will use the Hunter Tool Cutter to turn the project down to size and then switch to conventional HSS tools to complete the fine finish cuts."

However, in our shop tests, the #4 tool performed equally well in kiln-dried red oak, maple and hickory, as well as myrtlewood and walnut. It likes to skid a little until one gains some experience, but rotating the tool is like pressing the gas pedal and after a while it comes naturally. Tool testing is very subjective and all opinions are suspect, but our tester thought the Hunter cutter outperformed traditional bowl gouges (with fingernail grinds) in every aspect of performance.

J&B Tools

This, according to their Web site, is "a small company founded on the principle of low frills and high quality". Their goal is "to produce high quality American made woodturning tools that are affordable for all wood turners".

J&B offers three versions of carbide insert lathe tools: the Peeler (Photo 16), the Shaver and the Digger. The Peeler uses a flat 14mm square cutter and is available with or without a handle. It is 12" unhandled, or 24" overall with a 16" handle. It has a ½" square steel shaft, and is intended for convex curves and fast stock removal.

The Shaver takes a round 10mm saucer-shaped cutter and has a ½" round steel shaft. It is available in handled versions that are 18" and 24" overall, or 12" unhandled. A smaller version is also available with a ⅜" diameter shaft.

The Digger is the latest offering from J&B Tools, and it was designed for rough hollowing. It has a round 11mm carbide cutter on a round shaft, "to provide for both scrape cutting and shear scraping, depending on the angle the tool is presented to the wood". The company says this tool is "excellent for those situations where uneven grain or knots in your project make using a gouge frustrating. Also great for projects where the depth is greater than the diameter and a gouge just will not work. The Digger will work in all types of both side grain and end grain hollowing with a minimal fear of a catch."

The Shaver apparently delivers a cleaner surface than the Digger, and the carbide cutters on these tools are not interchangeable. The Digger is available in a ⅜" and also a ½" round steel shaft, with or without handles. The smallest versions of the Shaver and Digger are 9" un-handled and 18" with a handle.

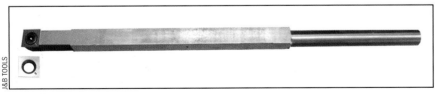

16 The 14mm square Peeler from J&B Tools is available with or without a handle.

Jewelwood Studios/Eliminator

Located in Bothell, Washington, this shop is owned and operated by turner Jack McDaniel. His goal in developing the Eliminator line of tools was to eradicate catches, tear-out, and sharpening, and "make it easy for beginners as well as experienced turners to turn out quality work, time after time".

The standard Eliminator is a hollowing tool made from ¾" steel with a ½" tenon on the handle end. The business end has a tapered point with a ⅜" round carbide insert (Photo 18). The tool has two flats that are intended to make it more stable and more versatile than similar tools with round shanks. If used correctly, McDaniel says that "it will leave you with a very fine finish that needs little or no sanding."

The cutter is saucer-shaped, rather than flat. And the tapered shaft allows the cutter to reach into some spots that other tools might have to miss. It also allows Jewelwood to mount the cutter on a hefty piece of ¾" diameter steel that reduces vibration and chatter.

Aimed at all skill levels, the Eliminator comes in three sizes. Beyond the standard tool, the Mini Eliminator is a hollowing/detailing tool made from ½" steel with a tapered point and a ¼" (6mm) carbide insert. It works great on small boxes and ornaments, and also works as a detailing tool. And the Mega Eliminator has a 12mm cutter bit (½"), is made from a 1" steel bar, and is 16" overall. It lets a turner hollow up to 13" deep without outriggers or other paraphernalia, and "is very stable and easy to use".

17 Jack McDaniel's "Eliminator" has flat spots on the bottom to reduce rolling on the rest.

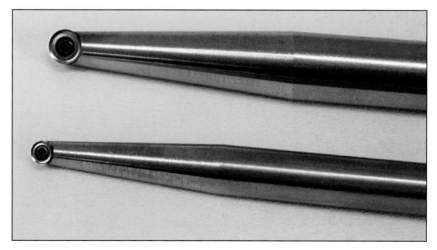

18 The standard Eliminator has a ⅜" cutter, and the Mini Eliminator's insert is ¼" diameter.

Mike Jackofsky's Hollow-Pro™ Tools

Designed by professional wood turner Mike Jackofsky, these unique tools are manufactured to his specs by Hunter Tools. They each have a flat shaft and a swivel head that holds the cutter at a negative angle. That is, the cutter can be moved left or right, and it slopes downward at a specific angle (negative means that it contacts the work at less than 90 degrees), to deliver the best cut with the lowest possibility of catches.

There are four tools in the series: two large and two small, and each pair is designed to handle different sized work. There is a straight tool and a bent tool with a ½" square shaft, and then the same again with ⅝" square shafts.

These tools have been specifically designed to use Hunter carbide cutters. The negative angle on the tools makes the carbide less aggressive and easier to control, which addresses the biggest problem that new turners have with saucer-shaped cutters. The tools remove wood quickly and efficiently from open bowls and hollow vessels.

Four carbide cutter assemblies are available. An assembly includes the cutter (insert) and the swiveling head that holds it.

RICK JACKOFSKY

19 There are four tools in the Hollow-Pro series, one of which has a bent shaft.

The #1 (⁷⁄₃₂") is for use on hard, dense woods and where limited stock removal is desired, and it works best with the ½" straight tool. The standard #2 (⁵⁄₁₆") cutter is for use on softer materials and where rapid stock removal is desired, especially when used with the ⅝" straight tool. The negative #2 cutter assembly has the cutter mounted at an additional negative angle (the swivel assembly is different),

20 Mike Jackofsky's tools have a swivel head that holds the cutter at a negative angle.

HOLLOW-PRO™ TOOLS

resulting in a less aggressive cut. It's recommended for both of the bent tools, and for lighter cuts with the straight tools. And finally, the #3 cutter is recommended only for light shaping and finishing cuts on open bowls.

The #1 and #2 negative cutter assemblies will work with any of the four tools; the standard #2 works best with the ⅝" straight tool; and the #3 is designed for use only in light cuts with the straight tools. In addition, all of the tools can accept a powdered metal scraper (M4), which is highly recommended for final finish cuts. These scrapers are the least aggressive cutters in the system, and are the easiest to use with all the tools.

The Hollow-Pro system is available from Craft Supplies USA, and there's a video on their Web site showing it in action. The swivel tip shafts and the scraper are all sold separately, and both the ½" and ⅝" tools are designed to fit into any large handle with a ⅝" opening.

New Edge Cutting Tools

Located in Plantsville, Connecticut, this company has developed carbide inserts since 2004. Their cutters are coated with a titanium nitride coating that is intended to create longer tool life at higher turning speeds. The concept is to produce smoother surfaces while maintaining a longer lasting, sharp, cutting edge.

New Edge inserts are saucer-shaped on the top surfaces, to create chip flow and that sharper cutting edge. Insert styles range from round to square and diamond shapes, and custom cutters can be ordered to meet specific profile needs.

Currently, the company offers ½", ¾" and 1" round cutters; a ¼" parting tool insert; a ¾" square cutter and a ½" diamond.

New Edge also sells an impressive pen turning system that is one tool with three carbide tips (straight, round and diamond), which also works well as a detailer on larger projects. The carbide cutters are bull-nosed for concave cuts; straight for convex and parting cuts; and triangular for detailing.

New Edge Cutting Tools are made in the USA.

21 New Edge's Inserts are round, square and diamond, and custom cutters can be ordered.

Rockler Woodworking and Hardware

Two carbide insert tools being sold exclusively by Rockler are available through their retail stores, catalog and Web site. These are a round tool (#42814) with a saucer-shaped cutter and a round shank, and a small square tool (#42281) with a flat cutter and a round shank.

The round tool has a 16" solid hardwood handle and brass ferrule, and the cutter was "sharpened on a diamond wheel of up to 1500 grit." The mini square tool has an 8" handle and is designed for "pens and other mini turning projects".

Of twelve customer reviews published on the Rockler site (8/23/11), there were three that gave the round tool 5 out of 5; three gave it 4 out of 5; three gave it 2 out of 5; and the final three gave it a score of 1 out of 5. There were no votes for 3 out of five, the average score. Positive reviews began with conditional comments such as "it took some practice to get the hang of using this tool" and "this can be a difficult tool to master". One noted that: "this tool is used much like a bowl gouge. First ride the bevel with the carbide at about 45 degrees from flat and rotate the handle until you start cutting." The same reviewer (who gave it 5 out of 5) said: "this is not like the 'easy' carbide tools".

The consensus seems to be that this is a great addition to the arsenal of relatively experienced turners who use it much like a bowl gouge, and it can be difficult for new turners to manage. The negative reviews said nothing bad about the quality of the tool, and most commented that the price was very fair. Their comments ran along the lines of: "I found this tool hard to control. The round shaft allows the tool (to) roll. It then digs into the wood. All cutting must be done within 5 degrees of straight on. The shaft needs a flat surface to ride on the tool rest, (to) stabilize the roll tendency."

With round shafts (combined with a round cutter that has sidewalls and a flat square cutter), it sounds like these tools might take a little experience to handle properly. But once mastered, their users seem to like them a lot.

ROCKLER WOODWORKING AND HARDWARE (2)

22 Rockler offers carbide insert tools with a flat square insert or a saucer-shaped round one.

Unique Tool/Things Western

Joe and Janet Rollings of Unique Tool in Rodeo, New Mexico offer a line of carbide tipped wood turning chisels that are 16½" long with cushioned, replaceable handles (actually, they are golf club grips!). The hardness of the carbide inserts is 91 on the Rockwell scale. Instructions are to "use flat like a scraper for shaping, then turn to an angle and sweep slowly as a shearing scraper for the finishing cut".

Unique tool guidelines say that these tools work well at high speeds and that "end grain cuts are smooth and free from catching and grabbing, unless you let the spindle speeds fall too low".

This company is unique in more than name. Joe Rollings wants users to resharpen their carbide cutters. "When it is dull all the way around," he says, "you can either sharpen it with a diamond file, take it to the saw shop, or return it to me for sharpening." They do sell replacement cutters, but only to customers who own their brand of tools.

In addition to the regular length (16½"), Unique Tool offers 24" and 36" long tools (this latter is called the "Boss Hogger"). And they also offer their ⅝" round shanks with a flat spot that is approximately ½" wide on the bottom, to better resist twisting in the hand when the cutter is used towards the side. The company makes three round tools (¾", ⅝", ½"), two squares (⅝" and ½"), and a ¾" triangle or "spear point". All six carbide inserts are flat, to avoid catches.

Unique Tool also offers a ½" square tool designed specifically for pen turners. They are only 10" long and have ½" shanks. The carbide inserts are the same grade as the larger chisels and are ½" round or ½" square. The bottoms of the shanks are flattened for the 2 inches directly under the insert.

23 Unique Tool's chisels have golf club grips and the hardness of the inserts is R-91.

Wood-of-1-Kind

Canadian Peter Cribari is a master pen maker who has turned to tool making. He sells two carbide insert lathe tools, the Skogger and the Rotondo. Both are made for pen turners, and are not intended to turn bowls. They both excel at spindle work. The tool shafts are made to his specifications by a top quality machine shop in Toronto. He turns a custom wooden handle for each tool, so no two are exactly alike. That's in keeping with the Wood-of-1-Kind corporate slogan: 'strive to be unique'.

"Every tool that I ship is personally inspected by me," Cribari says. "If it's not right, it doesn't leave my workshop. Of all the tools I have shipped, there hasn't been a single return."

The Skogger takes 15mm square solid carbide inserts. The steel shaft is 6" long, of which 2½" is the round tang that is inserted in the wood handle, and the handles range from 5" to 12" long. Wood-of-1-Kind provides either brass or copper ferrules to reinforce the custom turned wood handles. The ferrule safely holds the steel shaft within the wood handle and provides a secure grip. It is also intended to visually complement the wood.

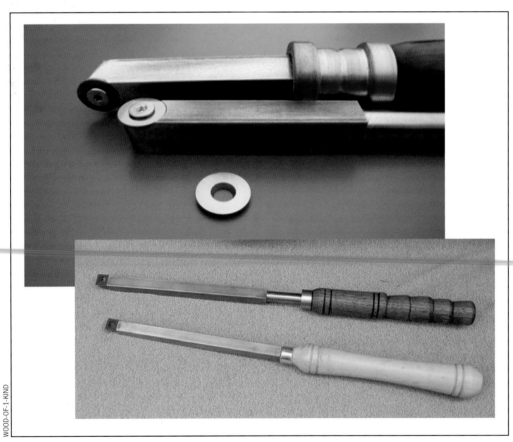

24 Wood-of-1-Kind sells two carbide insert lathe tools, the Skogger and the Rotondo.

Munro Tools Ltd.

While not strictly a carbide insert tool manufacturer, Rolly Munro does use some carbide cutters in his tools. He runs a turning studio in New Zealand, and during the summer of 2000 he was an ITE resident at the Woodturning Center in Philadelphia. One result of his personal journey through wood sculpture has been the invention of a set of hollowing tools, which he says on his Web site, "are pivotal in the creation of my hollow forms". His Munro Hollower is "the culmination of over thirty years of experimentation with designs for hollowing tools. It has been designed around a robust and inexpensive 12mm circular cutting tip, which I have coupled with a stainless steel depth gauge. The shaft of the tool is coupled with an aluminum handle, with a pleasingly tactile EVA grip. The tools have an articulated cutting head, allowing for hollowing around corners and under the shoulders of hollow forms." The cutter is either high-speed steel, or tungsten carbide, and both Packard Woodworks and Craft Supplies USA carry the hollower.

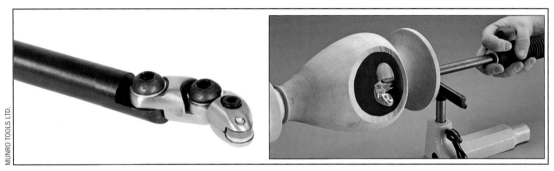

MUNRO TOOLS LTD.

25 The Munro Hollower has an articulated cutting head and HSS or carbide cutters.

Making Your Own Tools & Handles

Turners with a little knowledge of metalworking may want to visit the Web site of colorful Cap'n Eddie Castelin of Blackhawk Tools & Big Productions in Old Jefferson, Louisiana (eddiecastelin.com). Eddie has created numerous youtube.com videos covering various aspects of turning. View a complete listing of these by clicking on "Cap'n YouTube Gallery" on his site. Video #67 describes how to make ones own carbide insert tools (shafts and handles), and the Blackhawk Web site then sells the relevant carbide inserts, imported from Germany. The company provides one screw with each cutter. Available in the fall of 2011 were a 12mm round cutter (0226); a 15mm triangular cutting tool with three 60° angles; a 15mm diamond cutting tool with a 60° point; and a 14mm square cutting tool with square corners (below).

Blackhawk describes how to make ones own tools and sells the carbide inserts.

Blackhawk also sells shafts (which they call "bars"). These are crafted from mild steel, shaped and ground to accept the cutter, and then drilled and tapped to the proper screw size for the cutter. They are provided unfinished and un-handled. Bars are approximately 12" in length. There is a ⅜" round shaft for the round cutter, and a ½" square shaft that can be used with all of their other inserts.

Carbide Cutter Source

Bill McKnight of Carbide Depot in Birmingham, Alabama says his company specializes in metal cutting tools for the metal machining industry, but they have been receiving so many calls from turners looking for carbide inserts to use in wood that they now offer a line of round inserts and screws under their own brand name, Carbi-Universal. These can be found on their Web site at www.carbidedepot.com/wood-turning.htm, and include 8, 10 and 12mm diameters in ⅛", ⁵⁄₃₂" and ³⁄₁₆" heights.

Make Your Own Handles

At the Black Hills School of Woodworking, the staff has found that 16" to 30" long pieces of NPT ½" ID black gas pipe make great tool handles for carbide insert tools that have a ½" round shaft (facing page). Drill two ⁵⁄₃₂" holes near the business end (the length of the tool shaft will determine their locations) and tap

NPT ½" ID black gas pipe makes great handles for tools with a ½" round shaft.

these to receive 10-32 fine thread setscrews. Use ¼" long screws, so they don't stick up too high. If your hardware store uses Hillman as a supplier for all those small parts in the nut and bolt aisle (and most do), the Hillman stock # for 10-32 x ¼" fine thread setscrews is 777-E. They have an SAE thread and a cup point (tapered front end), and they take a ³⁄₃₂" hex wrench.

Insert the tool and lock it in place with the setscrews. Then stand at the lathe and hold the tool/handle as you would when turning. Note where your back hand (for most people, their right hand) is most comfortably located along the shaft. Wrap the shaft at that location with black Gorilla™ tape until it is thick enough to be comfortable (generally, this is about 1¼" in diameter.)

Complete the job by drilling a ⁵⁄₁₆" hole clear through the end of the handle, so it can be hung on the wall.

A Note of Caution from Toolmaker Peter Cribari

"Most of my clients turn pens to support themselves, as either a primary job or for secondary income. They don't mind paying for a good quality tool, but those who choose to make their own tools should be aware that what they create may lack proper tolerances, and can be rather unsafe. Unless the carbide insert is firmly seated on the solid steel handle, there is the possibility of the carbide shattering and becoming an airborne projectile—flying shrapnel if you will."

Web Sites:

Carbide Wood Turning Tools
http://carbidewoodturningtools.com

Easy Wood Tools
http://easywoodtools.com

Harrison Specialties
http://www.harrisonspecialties.com

Hunter Tool Systems
http://www.hunterwoodturningtool.com

J&B Tools
http://www.jandbtools.com

Jewelwood Studios/Eliminator
http://jewelwood.com/products

Mike Jackofsky's Hollow-Pro Tools
http://www.mikejackofsky.com/Tools.html

New Edge Cutting Tools
http://newedgecuttingtools.com

Rockler Woodworking and Hardware
http://www.rockler.com

Unique Tool/Things Western
http://www.thingswestern.com

Wood-of-1-Kind
http://wood-of-1-kind.webs.com/tools.htm

Munro Hollowing Tools
http://www.rollymunro.co.nz/tools.html

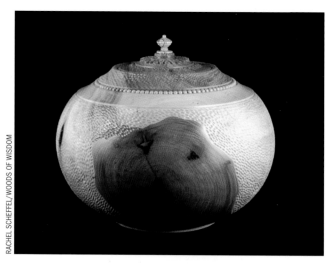

RACHEL SCHEFFEL/WOODS OF WISDOM

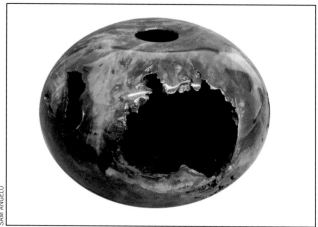

SAM ANGELO

CHAPTER 3

Technique: How to Use Carbide Tools

The shape of the cutter and the shape of the shaft both determine how a carbide insert lathe tool is used.

There are two shapes of carbide insert cutter. One is flat across the top, and the other is saucer or dish-shaped (Photo 1). Each of these requires a decidedly different approach when turning. Some companies use flat cutters for all of their profiles (round, square and triangular), while others prefer the saucer shape for their round inserts.

Regarding the shape of the shaft, there are, again, two families here: round ones, and square/rectangular ones (Photo 2). Some of the round shafts have flat bottoms, and these behave somewhat like square shafted tools.

In the following discussion, common lathe practices regarding things such as stance and safety issues are mentioned, but the focus is on how to use specific types of carbide insert tools. Notably absent from the conversation is any coverage of sharpening. And grain direction is also treated lightly, as it is not nearly as critical with carbide as it is with traditional tools.

1 The two types of round cutter are saucer-shaped (top) and flat-topped (bottom).

2 The tool shafts (between the cutting tip and the handle) can be square or round.

A Word about Lathe Speed

There are no hard and fast rules for how fast a work piece should be spinning on a lathe. But there are some common sense guidelines. When chucking an irregularly shaped piece that is out of round, for example, one must always start at the slowest speed. It's imperative that one tries to get the blank as balanced as possible (usually on the band saw) before mounting it for turning.

When using a new carbide insert tool for the first time, experiment at low speeds. Once one gets the "feel" of the tool, speeds can be increased. Most of the carbide insert manufacturers recommend mid-range to high speeds for final cuts, as this delivers a finer finish. Sanding works best at higher speeds, too. In fact, as long as the work is secure, sanding is usually done at the highest speed possible.

New turners tend to stay in the lower speed range for most of their projects, but if the work is stable and there's no vibration, they will find that they get a better cut as they dial up the speed. Experienced turners always match the speed to the project: large diameter work secured in a chuck calls for low initial speed (200 to 500 RPM), while small, secure projects between centers can often be turned at speeds up to 2,500 RPM and more.

Speed is also related to the size of the cutting tool. If large amounts of wood are being removed, a slower speed is usually called for. (An exception might be large spindle gouges.) Most lathe owner's manuals will list some kind of speed chart, and sometimes reading the manual is actually a good idea!

Dale Nish wrote a nice essay on lathe speeds and it has been posted on the Craft Supplies Web site (woodturnerscatalog.com). To read it, visit their home page and, about halfway down on the right, there's a box that says "Resource Center". Click

3 For stability, the shoulders of a blank in a chuck must make contact with the jaws.

on the word "Resources" and in the Woodturning Safety section click on "Safe Wood Lathe Speeds".

Whatever the speed, if it vibrates one must to turn off the lathe immediately, stand out of range of a possible projectile, find out why it's wobbling, and fix it. That may require a trip to the band saw, or remounting the work in a chuck or on a faceplate. One common cause of vibration for new turners is that their tenon is too long for the chuck (Photo 3), and the shoulders are not seated. In that case, it's quite likely that the tenon will snap and the bowl will go airborne.

Always keep in mind that old workshop adage—if it feels unsafe, it probably is.

Square Shafts and Flat-Topped Inserts

Lathe tools with square or rectangular shafts are designed to lie flat on the tool rest (Photo 4). The shaft shape is designed to help prevent the tool rolling when it's making side cuts. When a cutter is pushed straight into the wood, rolling isn't as much of an issue. But when hollowing a bowl or vessel, the side of the cutter often contacts the sidewall of the spinning work (Photo 5), and that can cause the tool to catch and rotate counterclockwise. If the

4 Lathe tools with square or rectangular shafts are designed to lie flat on the tool rest.

5 When hollowing, the side of a cutter can contact the sidewall of the spinning work.

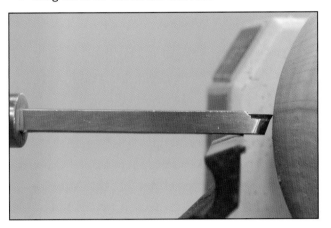

6 The cutting edge of flat-topped tools must be centered on the work and parallel to the floor.

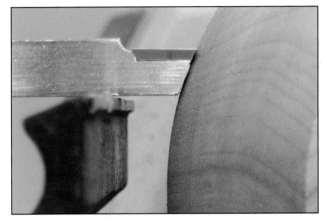

7 If the lathe's tool-rest is set too high, the cutter doesn't make contact with the work.

bottom of the shaft is flat, this reduces the amount of torque, and thus the propensity to roll. The wider the shaft, the more of it is in contact with the tool rest, and that also can help reduce torque.

Tools with flat cutters and flat-bottomed shafts are supposed to be centered on the work (Photo 6). That is, the tool rest height is adjusted so that the cutting edge of the tool (not the tool rest) can be lined up with the point of a live center that has been chucked in the tailstock. This is when the tool is held parallel to the floor and, because it is held at 90 degrees to the work, tools with flat cutters are said to be at a neutral angle. That is, one doesn't need to hold them at a negative or positive angle where the back end of the tool is kept either lower or higher than the cutting edge.

If the tool rest height is set so that the cutting edge is higher than center, the undercut (the bevel on the bottom of the cutter) may touch the work before the cutting edge, and the tool won't cut (Photo 7). The higher one goes above center, the less it cuts. If the tool is lower than center, the cutter will work to a degree (until it is too low), and it may catch and drag. Many turners who have a tall lathe or who are of shorter stature themselves tend to set the tool rest a little low and then hold the tool on a slant with the back end low. The net result (hopefully) is that their cutter is actually centered. Avoid cutting above center on the outside of a bowl, or below center on the inside of one, because catches are more likely.

8 Before turning on the lathe, rotate work by hand to see that the wood clears the tool-rest .

9 The leading edge of a flat tool rest should be about ½" away from the wood.

Keep in mind that the cutting edge, and not the top of the tool rest, must be centered. With the thick shafts on many carbide insert tools, the top of the tool rest can be as much as ⅝" lower than center. If all of your tools have the same shaft thickness, it's a good idea to attach a hose clamp to the tool rest post, so that it's always on center when dropped into the banjo.

With the tool rest height established for a flat shaft, the next step is to locate the banjo (the metal base that holds the tool rest). This determines how far the tool rest will be from the work, and its location depends a lot on the way the cutting tool is built. The first step here is to make sure it's not too far forward. With the power turned off, slowly rotate the work by hand and make sure that the wood clears the tool rest (Photo 8). Then move the banjo back (increasing the distance between the work and the tool rest) until the flat bottom of the tool shaft is fully supported by the rest when the cutter meets the wood.

On longer tools, experienced turners may cantilever the tool a little and have more of it in front of the rest than is safe with short handled tools. The best balance, however, is to keep the rest as close as possible to the work while still fully supporting the tool. With most flat shafts, the leading edge of a flat tool rest (as opposed to a cylindrical one) will be about ½" away from the wood (Photo 9). That's just an estimate, and a turner should always follow the lathe and the tool manufacturers' guidelines. It's a good idea to use a rest that is shaped to reach around the bowl or vessel, and provide support close to the cut. On wide-necked vessels and bowls, the inexpensive "Penetrator" from thingswestern.com is a popular solution for this. For outside curves, various bent and curved rests are widely available (Photo 10).

With cylindrical rather than flat tool rests, the fulcrum (the highest point of the cylinder) supports the tool, so that needs to be considered when setting the banjo. The front of the cylinder should be perhaps ⅛" to ¼" away from the wood, for maximum support (Photo 11). If the tool catches in the wood, the violence of the catch is directly related to how much of the tool extends past the supporting tool rest. That's why experienced turners are constantly adjusting their rests inward as they remove stock.

The tool rest should *never* be adjusted while the work is still spinning.

10 Curved tool-rests wrap around work and provide continuous support for sweeping cuts.

11 On round tool-rests, the fulcrum (pivot point) is usually a little bit farther back from the work.

12 Easy Wood Tools recommend anchoring the end of the handle close against one's body.

13 It's a good idea to keep a new, sharp insert handy for the last couple of clean-up passes.

Craig Jackson of Easy Wood Tools (who makes square shafted tools with flat-topped inserts) insists that keeping his tools flat on the tool rest is not just a recommendation, but is actually a requirement for safety and proper performance as one learns this new way to turn.

"Even a very slight rotation of the tool from flat will reduce performance and safety," he says. "If you find the tool is unstable during a cut, stop cutting and reposition the tool flat on the rest. Then relax your back handle grip, and apply firm thumb pressure to hold the front of the tool on the rest. Use the hand that grips the handle to maintain the tool level."

"Our turners find it helpful to position the handle level at the beginning of a cut, and then bring it close to their body, to provide an anchor point (Photo 12). As they turn, they may begin to forget about keeping the tool level, and touching it against their body seems to help with that. If they start to have trouble with the stability of a cut, they are advised to immediately stop cutting and reposition the tool level to the floor."

When using flat-topped inserts in tools with flat shafts, there are a couple of things that will help make final cuts extremely clean. The first is to keep a new, sharp insert handy and switch to this for the last couple of passes (Photo 13). Then switch back

14 To get a clean cut in difficult grain, use just the leading corner of the Rougher.

to the regular insert for the next hogging job. This maximizes the use one gets from a pair of inserts. When all of the fine edges of the finishing insert begin to fade, simply make that one of the hogging ones, and use a new cutter for final passes. With such light usage, the finishing insert will last a long, long time.

The second key to a great finish cut is to take one's time. The final couple of passes need to be done very slowly. That is, the cutter needs to travel slowly across the work.

Jackson also has some advice for getting a clean cut in difficult grain. He suggests using just the leading corner of the cutter on an Easy Rougher (the square insert tool), with the tool presented at about 15 degrees to the travel of the cut. The front edge near the corner cuts and the tip (middle of the cutter) stays in slight contact with the wood trailing the cut (Photo 14).

Easy Wood Tools recommends that one avoid over-tightening the screws that lock inserts into the tools. They need to be firmly secured, but the hex wrench should be used "…to lightly hand tighten the screw. This will provide adequate force

to secure your cutter. Rest assured, the design of the tool system will hold the cutter securely with minimal hex wrench torque."

The company also advises lightly greasing cutter screw threads when a new insert is installed, especially when turning in green wood. And they suggest that a turner should thoroughly clean out the hex socket of the screw before inserting a hex wrench. This allows the wrench to make full contact with the screw, and will prevent stripping out the hex socket.

Peter Cribari of Wood-of-1-Kind designs tools for pen turners that, like EWT, are optimized at the center of the pen blank. In other words, the carbide insert faces the pen blank at its midpoint. For these short tools, the cutter must be advanced towards the rotating blank with the smallest possible clearance between the tool rest and the work.

"The smaller the gap, the less chance there is of a catch," Cribari says. "Some turners refer to this technique as 'riding on the level.'"

The cutters used by Wood-of-1-Kind have a bevel on the edge of 75 degrees. This is a lot more than metalworking carbide inserts, which only have about 30 degrees of bevel. That makes them unable to turn wood and acrylic, which is why some turners have historically held some negative views of the cutting abilities of wood-cutting carbide inserts. They are, Cribari notes, two totally different types of insert for two totally different applications.

Square Shafts and Saucer-shaped Inserts

Many of the techniques espoused by Craig Jackson for Easy Wood Tools also apply to Mike Jackofsky's line of Hollow-Pro tools. These, too, have a square

15 Mike Jackofsky tools have a swivel head that holds the cutter at a pre-set angle.

HOLLOW-PRO TOOLS

shaft that uses the tool rest to help control rolling. However, Hollow-Pro tools use saucer-shaped, round carbide inserts. To avoid catches and achieve the optimum cut, Jackofsky has eliminated much of the guesswork in holding the tool at the correct angle. The tips of his tools have a swivel head that holds the cutters at an angle (Photo 16), so the turner just needs to concentrate of keeping the shaft flat on the rest.

As with Easy Wood Tools, the height of the tool rest for Hollow-Pro tools should be adjusted so that when the tool is held straight (parallel to the bed of the lathe) the tip is cutting at the centerline of the turning.

"For less aggressive cuts," Jackofsky says, "raise the handle slightly. Avoid lowering the handle, as that will raise the cutter tip and could result in a very aggressive angle of cut." Both companies recommend holding the handle against your body, and Jackofsky adds that one should practice with the tools on an open bowl before using them on a hollow vessel.

There are two types of tools in the Hollow-Pro system – straight and bent (swan neck). The bent hollowing tools are held manually (without a jig) and, as with the swan neck tools from Easy Wood,

it's important that the straight part of the shaft lies on the tool rest (Photo 16). If the curved portion is on the tool rest, a catch will twist the handle from the turner's grasp. It's very important to keep the handle level, so that the cutter won't be raised and try to make cuts that are too aggressive. As there are two sizes available, the company advises using the smaller tool to start work on bigger projects, as the shorter swan neck offers more support in initial passes.

16 It's important that the straight part of a swan neck tool's shaft lies on the tool-rest.

Choosing the right tip (the part that holds the cutter at a set angle) is an important part of the process when using Hollow-Pro tools.

"All the different tips fit all the tools," Jackofsky says, "but I like the standard #1 cutter assembly for the ½" straight tool, the standard #2 cutter assembly for the ⅝" straight tool and the #2 negative cutter assembly for both of the bent tools. But I also use negative cutter assemblies, which are less aggressive, for finish cuts with the straight tools as well." He recommends the ⅝" straight tool for open bowls as well as hollow forms, and suggests that beginning turners might start with the straight tools, as they're easy to use.

"If you make shapes with a big enough opening," he says, "you can do all the hollowing with straight tools. But if you get into making smaller openings, or more difficult shapes, you will need bent tools as well.

Tools with Round Shafts

There are several manufacturers using saucer-shaped inserts in round-shafted tools. Mike Hunter of Hunter Tools in Minneapolis is a leader in this field. His Web site has several videos online that explain the required technique, and it's all about bevels and angles. Imagine if the tool was held so that the top of the screw holding the cutter was facing the ceiling. If we call that position 12 o'clock, then rotating the tool 90 degrees counterclockwise would bring the insert to 9 o'clock.

The saucer-shaped round cutter on a Hunter tool sits on a steel shaft. The tip of that shaft has a bevel that runs from the top to the bottom. When a cut is started, the tool is held on the rest so that it is parallel to the floor, and the shaft is rotated so the cutter is at about 9:00. Then, the end of the handle is swung to the right a little until the bevel under

17 With saucer-shaped cutters, begin with the bevel under the cutter parallel to the wood.

18 Without rotating it, the handle is moved to the left until the cutter makes contact.

the cutter is parallel to the wood (Photo 17). At this point, the tool is moved in until the bevel is actually rubbing the wood but no cutting is happening. Now, without rotating it, the end of the handle is slowly swung to the left until the cutting edge just barely makes contact (Photo 18). Once there, the shaft can be rotated slightly to the right (toward 10 o'clock and even beyond) to increase the amount of wood being removed (Photo 19).

In other words, one rides the bevel until the tool begins to cut, and then moves away from the bevel

19 The shaft is then rotated clockwise to increase the amount of wood being removed.

20 Best cuts seem to be achieved when the cutter rotation is between 10 and 11 o'clock.

and rotates the cutter slowly into the wood. Best cuts are achieved when the rotation is between 10 and 11 o'clock (in the neighborhood of 45 degrees) (Photo 20). This tool will catch more as it nears 12 o'clock.

It sounds complicated, and it does take a project or two to get comfortable with the technique, but once mastered, it's quite efficient and the resulting surface is very satisfying. Cuts can be made traveling left or right (Photo 21). New turners need to remember to keep the tool closed (closer to 9 o'clock than 12). Open it too much, and it will catch.

An experienced turner, John Lucas, demonstrates Hunter Tools on their Web site. During one of his videos, he says: "Although you can hollow a complete bowl with these tools, I find its best use is on final cuts. I'll rough out with a bowl gouge because I think it's a little more efficient, and then I'll use the Hunter Tools for the final cuts."

Fred Holder of More Woodturning has a review of the Hunter line on his Web site, and he used only these tools to make an end-grain box and

21 Very clean cuts can be made traveling left or right with a saucer-shaped cutter.

a side-grain bowl. On the box, he said: "The tool cut away the center of the piece quickly and cleanly. I didn't make a hole first, but I believe this would make it work even better. I then tried the tool on the outside of the little box I was working on. It cut cleanly without the catch that I had expected. The wood was ready to sand after the cut down the outside. I was impressed with this tool. It not only hollowed end grain, but cut side grain as well."

Flattened Round Shafts

A variant on the round shaft/round cutter is Jack McDaniel's Eliminator. This tool has a tapered round shaft with two flat spots ground on the bottom. One of these holds the cutter at 45 degrees to the left, and the other at 45 degrees to the right. (Photo 22)

"This tool is easier to use with a draw (pulling) cut," McDaniel says, "but it can be used pushing or pulling without fear of the deadly catches. Generally, I start with a drilled center hole (⅜") to gauge the total depth of the vessel, but it's not required. Just start in the middle of the vessel with the tool on the centerline, put the flat of the tool on the tool rest and sweep the cutter head toward the rim, keeping a light pressure downward on the tool rest. Keeping the flat of the tool on the tool rest gives you an automatic 45-degree slant for the cutter, and allows you to make smooth sweeping cuts. This is not a scraper: it cuts very clean shavings, not sawdust.

"The tool is designed with two flats on the barrel that lay on the tool rest. When you are running your lathe in the forward direction, use the flat that tilts the tool to the left for a pull or pull cut. If running in reverse, just reverse the procedure by using the other flat."

If possible, use two tool-rests (which requires buying a second banjo for your lathe), as this adds immensely to the stability of hollowing tools. Place one very close to the work and slide the second banjo snug up against the first. Then press down between the two rests while hollowing (Photo 23). The heights need to be adjusted so that the cutting edge is centered on the work.

JACK MCDANIEL

22 The Eliminator has flat spots on the bottom that hold the cutter at 45° left or right.

23 One can dramatically increase stability in deep work with a second banjo and tool-rest.

Technique is obviously related to shafts and cutters, and most manufacturers have Web sites that explain the niceties of their own individual designs. My personal opinion is that flat-topped cutters installed on wide, flat shafts are ideal for beginning to intermediate turners, while round cutters with saucer-shaped inserts seem best suited to turners who are familiar with riding bevels and making inside and outside shear cuts with bowl gouges. Somewhere in between are saucer-shaped cutters on square shafts.

CHAPTER 4

Turning Between Centers

Project 1: A Hickory Candlestick

This project is a great introduction to a new set of carbide insert lathe tools. It could be executed in walnut, maple or almost any other hardwood, but hickory turns beautifully and is quite handsome.

There are two ways to turn: between centers (along the grain), and using a faceplate or chuck (across the grain). This project includes both methods, and it also addresses inside and outside (concave and convex) curves. The base diameter is 4¾" and the finished piece stands 11" tall.

The phrase 'turning between centers' simply means that one end of the work is attached to the headstock of the lathe, and the other is attached to the tailstock. The powered point in the headstock is called a drive center (or spur drive), and the freely spinning point in the tailstock is known as a live center. Hence, the work is 'between centers'. Work held in this position has its grain running parallel to the bed of the lathe, so the turner is always moving a cutting tool into side grain (as opposed to end grain). As the most popular project done between centers is to create stair, chair and railing spindles, turning this way has also come to be known as spindle turning.

Make a Cylinder

Begin the project by cutting a 2" square blank to 10" in length. On the drill press, drill a ⅞" diameter hole ⅞" deep, centered

1 Drill a ⅞" hole for the candle and use this to locate the tailstock's live center.

Traditionally, the first tool that a turner would reach for was a spindle gouge. This large, U-shaped tool is used to reduce a square blank to a cylinder. With a little practice, this can be a very quick operation, but new turners often have reservations about pushing such a huge tool into a spinning piece of wood.

Set the lathe speed somewhere between 800 and 1,000 RPM (each lathe is different, but this will probably be the second slowest available speed).

You will be using a roughing tool (the standard one in our shop is the Ci1 square rougher from Easy Wood Tools), to start. With flat carbide inserts, the tool should be held parallel to the floor, and you should have a solid but not severe grip on the end of the handle. Tuck the tool against your body: this helps prevent our natural tendency to drop the end of the handle lower than it should be. A right-handed turner will have the index finger of his/her left hand against the tool rest, and the thumb firmly on top of the tool's shaft.

Begin at one end of the blank and gently move the cutter into the wood until it makes contact. Don't push too deeply. Keep in mind that, because it's a square, the cutting edge will hit wood, then air, and then wood again, so there will be some mild chatter. Slowly slide the cutter sideways: the edges of carbide inserts cut just as keenly as the fronts. Move along the whole length of the work, taking a very slight cut. The tool handle should be at 90 degrees to the work, so remember to slide your body, not just your wrists, to maintain this angle.

Repeat the procedure, taking very slight cuts until you are comfortable with the process. Then shut off the power and check that everything is tight on the lathe. If the cutter has momentarily stopped the work spinning, the live center in the tailstock needs to be wound in more, to drive the wood more firmly onto the drive center.

in one end. This will be for the candle, so it's the top of the project. Most standard live centers (the freely spinning one in the tailstock) will fit into this opening rather snuggly. A large, cone-shaped live center works, too (Photo 1).

On the other end of the blank, find center by drawing two diagonal lines from opposite corners. Where they cross is the center of the blank. Drill a small hole (about ⅛" diameter x ¼" deep works), and seat the sharp point of the drive center in this. Using a small piece of scrap wood to protect the top of the candlestick, tap the blank with a mallet or hammer until the teeth on the drive center are engaged. Slide the tailstock up until the live center is seated in the hole for the candle, and lock the tailstock in place. Wind the live center forward until it seems quite secure, and then lock that adjustment, too. Set the tool rest so that the cutting edge of the tool is centered on the wood. Manually rotate the blank to make sure it doesn't hit the tool rest: it should be perhaps ¼" from the closest part of the wood. Find your safety glasses (although a face shield is a *much* better option), make sure you have enough light, check that somebody knows you're in the shop, and you're ready to turn.

2 Use the Rougher to reduce the blank to the largest diameter cylinder that it will make.

3 Stay with the rougher to mill a tenon for the chuck on the bottom of the candlestick.

4 Dismount the blank to test fit the tenon in a hole the size of the one you will drill in the base.

5 Remount the blank on the lathe, this time locking the tenon into a 4-jaw chuck.

Once everything is tight, proceed with the process. Occasionally stop the lathe to visually check progress. With the power off, manually turn the wood looking for flat spots. Some people prefer to move left to right (Photo 2), others right to left, and some work in both directions. Whatever is comfortable and feels safe is right.

Add Some Shape

When the blank has been reduced to a cylinder, the next step is to create a tenon on the bottom so that the candlestick can eventually be attached to its base. The tenon is made with a square cutter that is simply pushed in slowly until the correct diameter has been reached (Photo 3). The base will be drilled with a 35mm (or 1⅜") Forstner bit to accept this tenon, so it's a good idea to drill a hole in some scrap and dry fit the tenon (Photo 4). I also like to undercut the shoulder. That is, I create a very slight cone shape on the bottom of the candlestick so that, when it is secured to the base, only the edges touch and it looks like a really tight fit.

If a chuck is available, remove the spur drive from the lathe and replace it with this more secure option (Photo 5). This step is not critical.

6 Begin forming the bottom of the candlestick using the Rougher to create the outside curve.

7 Use a round Finisher to create the two arcs that form the bulb above the bottom.

8 Stay with the Finisher to mill the cove between the bottom curve and the bulb.

9 Use a Detailer to cut a thin groove where the cove meets the bottom curve.

Move the end of the square cutter's handle to the right and use the corner of the cutter to create a V-shaped cut that is centered an inch to the right of the tenon. Then slowly swing the cutter through the left-hand corner of the cut, rounding it over. This creates a convex curve (Photo 6). The key here is to sweep the end of the handle from right to left in one smooth motion at the cutter travels around the curve.

Now use a ½" round carbide insert to create two deep concave cuts along the body of the candlestick. Between them, you'll see a bulb shape emerge (Photo 7).

Stay with the round tool to create a small cove just above the convex curve (Photo 8). At the bottom of this short arc, use a detailer to score a shallow groove (Photo 9), and then burn a black line in the groove with a wire (Photo 10). This is a shop-built jig and the wire has a short wooden handle on each end. The trick is to stretch it tight in the groove and hold it there until it begins to smoke. Then hold on for about five more seconds. Wires can be quite dangerous if they get wrapped up in the spinning work.

The top of the candlestick has a round ball sitting atop a mushroom. Where they meet, use the corner

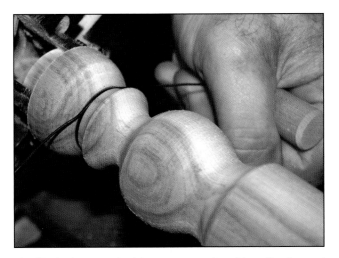

10 A wire stretched between two dowel handles is used to burn the decorative black line.

11 Begin shaping the top of the candlestick by cutting a deep V with the Rougher.

12 Finish turning the ball and its V-shaped shoulder using the square Rougher.

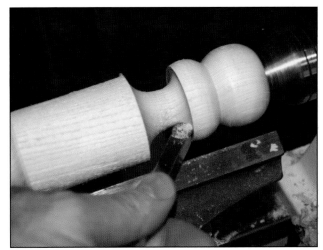

13 A small round carbide insert is ideal for undercutting the bottom of the mushroom.

of the square tool to create a V (Photo 11). Then slowly round over both sides of the V, moving the end of the handle in sync with the cutter's travel around each arc. On the ball, the same tool is used to round over the top edge, too (Photo 12).

Fashion the underside of the mushroom with the round tool (Photo 13), still keeping the shaft parallel to the floor. Note that the leading edge of the cutter is approaching the work at 90 degrees. That is, the part of the tool doing the work is the front, and not the sides of the cutter. When making an undercut like this, there is less chance of chatter if the tool handle is swung around to create the

arc (so that the middle of the insert almost always meets the wood), rather than simply reaching in and pushing the cutter from left to right. While the sides will definitely cut, using the leading edge allows the shock of impact to be driven down a straight line through the cutter to the tool handle, down to the tool rest, and then into the mass of the lathe, which is better than having vibrations running up your arms.

The square tool with a slightly radiused cutter is ideal for creating the gradual sweep between the mushroom and the bulb (Photo 14). If a cutter

14 The long, gradual sweep can be formed with a Rougher and cleaned up with a Finisher.

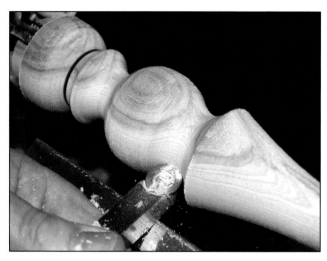

15 Refine the transition between the bulb and the sweep using a round Finisher.

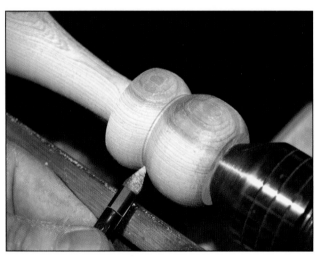

16 Cut the shallow groove between the ball and the mushroom using a Detailer.

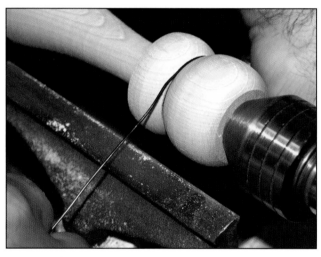

17 Once more, use a wire to burn the decorative black line in the groove.

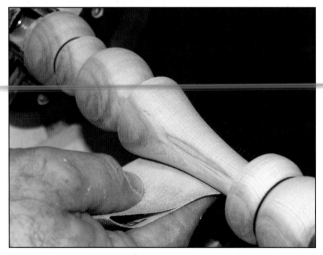

18 With the lathe speed turned up (check everything is tight), sand down through the grits.

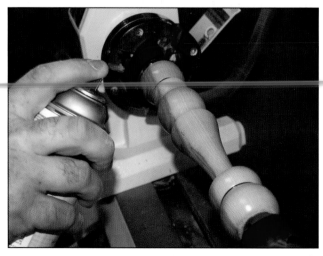

19 Mask the machine parts, open a window or two, and apply the finish of your choice.

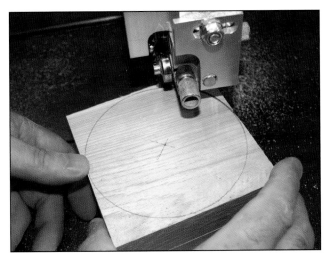

20 Draw diagonal lines to find center on the base, draw a circle, and then bandsaw it to size.

21 True the blank for the base (make it perfectly round) after mounting it on a faceplate.

with a radius isn't available, the round tool can handle this job.

Use the round tool to clean up the two shallow spots on either side of the bulb, creating clean, sharp edges at the outsides (Photo 15). The trick here is to take very shallow cuts and move the tool very slowly across the wood. The edges don't need to be knife-edges: they'll be sanded later on, and can be 'sharpened' then.

Score a line where the mushroom meets the ball, using the detailer (Photo 16), and then burn the line with wire (Photo 17). Sand down through the grits from 120 to 180, 220, 280 and 320 (Photo 18), running the lathe at its highest speed. Then switch to the lowest speed and, with the lathe turned off, mask the chuck and tailstock. Open plenty of doors and windows, and then spray several light coats of quick-drying lacquer as the work is spinning (Photo 19). Let each coat dry, and sand between coats with 400-grit sandpaper.

Make the Base

The candlestick base begins with a 4½" square block of 6/4 hickory. The thickness of hardwood is described in quarter-of-an-inch increments, when

the wood is still rough. So, a 1" thick board is 4/4 (four quarter), a two-inch thick piece of stock is 8/4 (eight quarter), and so on. Note that it isn't 4/4". Those two little hash marks behind the last digit that denote an inch are reserved for planed boards.

The base of the candlestick is 1½" thick, and it can be made by face gluing two pieces of ¾" thick stock together. Be sure the grain runs the same way in both, or they will expand and contract in different directions and the glue bond may fail.

Draw a 4⅜" diameter circle centered on one face of the blank, and band saw to this line (Photo 20). Screw a scrap block to a faceplate and then use hot melt glue to attach the hickory blank for the base to the scrap. Bring up the tailstock and lock it in place. Then use the large round cutter to true up the blank and make it round (Photo 21). While the manufacturer calls this tool a Finisher, it works extremely well on small rounds that have alternating side grain and end grain. Note that the tailstock is in place, to add support.

Switch to the straight tool to round over the top edge of the base, again swiveling the back end of the handle to keep pace with the cutter (Photo 22).

22 The profile of the base begins with the creation of two outside curves, or shoulders.

23 Use the left edge of the Rougher to define and shape the top curve.

24 Use the right edge of the Rougher to define and shape the bottom curve.

25 The round-nosed Finisher does a nice job of creating a stepped cove in the top curve.

Stay with the straight tool to define the top of the step (Photo 23). If your blank was two boards face glued together, you can make the glue line disappear here by cutting the "L" in the step to line up with the glue line. The bottom of the step is simply rounded over and this, too, is completed with the square cutter (Photo 24).

Go back to the round tool to create the cove above the step (Photo 25), and then gently shape the top of the base (from the candlestick to the edge) with a gentle slope. Install a drill chuck in the tailstock, chuck a 35mm bit in it, and drill the round mortise for the tenon on the end of the candlestick spindle (Photo 26). Then sand and finish the base in place, and glue and clamp the two parts together when the finish is dry.

26 Slow the lathe to its lowest speed before using a Forstner bit to drill the hole for the tenon.

CHAPTER 5

Basic Bowl Turning with Flat Cutters

Project 2: A Mixed Species Bowl

Bowls are the first thing we think of when we hear the word "turning". And skills gained while making bowls transfer to more challenging projects (hollow vessels, for example), as our expertise expands. In this chapter are guidelines for making two projects: a basic open bowl, and a lidded, shaped one. The first of these builds some skills that make it easier to tackle the second. Both are made here with flat-topped cutters in square shafted tools.

Working in kiln-dried hardwoods often requires that a turner laminate two or three layers of stock together to create a blank that is thick enough for bowl turning. That's because it's very difficult to kiln dry thick boards, as the outside dries so much faster than the core. Hence, there is plenty of thinner stock on the market, and thick boards are at a premium. This can actually be an advantage, because a turner can combine two or more species and create something with more life and color.

In this case, a layer of 8/4 red oak has been laminated to one of 4/4 black walnut. This delivers a small oak bowl with a dramatic walnut rim. (For more on the glue-up process, see the lidded bowl project, below.) After the glue dries, draw a 5" diameter circle on the blank using a compass and then band saw the part to a circle. Use the same fulcrum (the pinpoint made by the compass) to

1 Glue up a two-species blank, bandsaw it round, and draw a circle for the faceplate.

2 Pre-drill pilot holes for sheetmetal screws, center the plate and drive them home.

3 True up the blank using a straight cutter, keeping the tailstock engaged for safety.

4 Stay with the straight cutter to begin shaping the outside curve of the bowl.

draw another circle just larger than your faceplate (Photo 1), and this makes it very easy to center the plate on the blank. Attach the plate to the blank with sheet metal screws driven into pre-drilled holes (Photo 2). Sheetrock screws are brittle and may break under strain.

Mount the faceplate on the headstock of the lathe, and then draw up the tailstock. Any time you can use the tailstock to stabilize a blank, it's advisable to do so. Set the speed for about 1,000 RPM and use a carbide-tipped roughing tool (the square one) to gradually true the blank. This is done in small increments (Photo 3), starting with the cutting

edge located about halfway onto the blank. Move the tool gently into the spinning wood, expecting it to chatter very slightly because the blank is not yet perfectly round. The cutting edge will make contact, then be in a small void, and then make contact again. When the chatter disappears, the blank is true.

Next, create the convex curve on the outside of the bowl. As the cutter removes stock along this arc, the end of the handle must keep pace. That is, the entire tool needs to swivel (Photo 4), not just the cutting edge.

5 Chucks usually come with a set of inside (shown installed on the lathe) and outside jaws.

6 Use the straight cutter to create a tenon for the chuck on the bottom of the bowl blank.

To be able to reach the inside of the bowl, the blank needs to be reversed and mounted in a chuck. This can be a relatively inexpensive accessory (they start at about $80), and it's pretty much essential for good work. Some turners get by with gluing blocks of scrap wood to their blanks and then cutting these away, but a basic self-centering utility chuck is ideal for almost any size turning. They are opened and closed with a single hex key, or else with two short steel rods. The keyed ones generally cost more, and they have no major advantage other than convenience. If you slide the tailstock up to keep the blank in place while it is being secured in the jaws of a chuck, both of your hands are then free to hold the rods. Four jaws are generally a better idea than three, because they will accommodate square stock for spindles, finials and other work between centers.

Most chucks come with both inside and outside (#1 and #2) jaws (Photo 5). The #1 step jaws can be used to hold a tenon, or they can be expanded inside a round mortise (a hole drilled or turned in the bottom of the bowl). The thinner #2 jaws work best in a mortise. Bowl turners generally favor tenons because this method uses up less of the blank, allowing for a deeper bowl.

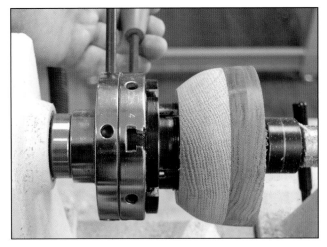

7 Lock the tenon in the chuck. Note that the tailstock has again been engaged for safety.

Mill the tenon with a square roughing tool (Photo 6), paying special attention to its dimensions. The jaws on a chuck form a perfect circle when they are almost closed, and that's the best diameter for a tenon. The jaws will leave the smallest imprint then, and will have the best grip possible.

The tenon also needs to be long enough to allow the jaws to get a good grip, but short enough that it doesn't bottom out. It's absolutely crucial that the shoulders of the tenon are snug against the outside edges of the jaws. That is, the entire tenon must be inside the jaws, without touching bottom (Photo 7). Note that the live center in the tailstock is used

8 Secure the tool rest in front of the piece, and use the straight cutter to square up the face.

9 Starting just off-center, begin hollowing with the round insert, working outward in steps.

10 Be careful not to go too deep in the center of the bowl, or you'll cut into the tenon.

to push the blank into the chuck, so that it sits flush as the jaws are tightened.

When the blank is secure, slide the tailstock out of the way. Then locate the tool rest and lock it in place. Manually rotate the chuck, to make sure nothing hits the tool rest. Then switch on the lathe and begin milling the inside by flattening the face (Photo 8). This, again, can be one with the roughing tool.

Switch to a finisher (the round cutter) to hollow the inside of the bowl. Begin in the center and work out to the edges (Photo 9). This allows you to "drill" a hole in the center and then gradually

expand it. The hole is not full depth. Go about ¾" deep, work about half the way out to the edge, and then come back and drill a little deeper at the center, creating steps (Photo 10). This method leaves as much mass as possible for as long as possible on the sidewalls, lending them stability. Traditional turners using a fluted bowl gouge prefer to cut close to the edge and work their way into the center. In fact, they often drill out the center to full depth first, and then peel the walls. Flat-topped carbide insert tools have such a low propensity to catch that they simplify many of the traditional techniques, which means that they sometimes end up being used in ways that traditional turners might consider counterintuitive.

As more of the waste is removed, the cutting tool creates a space where a curved tool rest can be used to support the cutter closer to the work (Photo 11). Remember to swing the end of the tool handle when working on the sidewalls so that most of the downward force is concentrated closer to the middle of the cutter than the left edge. This will essentially eliminate the tool's tendency to roll counterclockwise. Reduce the walls to about ⅜" thickness. Your final pass should be very slow, to deliver a clean surface.

11 A curved tool-rest is ideal for hollowing bowls, as the end can be moved in to give support.

12 To create the impression that the walls are thinner than they are, mill a cove around the lip.

Now, here's a trick of the trade. By creating a small cove on the outside edge of the bowl, the rim appears much lighter (Photo 12). This gives the impression that the sidewalls are thinner than they actually are. Note that the tool rest has been moved to perform this task, and that the front edge of the cutter is being used to remove the waste.

Sand the inside and outside of the bowl down through the grits (100, 180, 220, 280 and 320) before removing it from the chuck. This is usually done at the lathe's top speed. If possible, rig up a dust collection hose, or at least provide lots of ventilation and a dust mask. Keep the paper moving, or it will dig deep furrows around your bowl. Whenever possible, fold the paper twice to allow four thicknesses, or it will quickly become too hot to handle. Remove the tool rest, to avoid trapping your fingers.

Chuck manufacturers offer several different types of jaws for their chucks, and one of the most popular options is a set of flat jaws (Photo 13). These hold the bowl by its rim, allowing the turner to remove the tenon and clean up the bottom. It's a good idea to run a strip of blue masking tape around the bowl, to protect it from the soft rubber

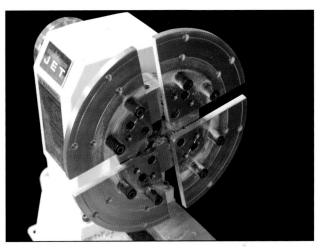

13 Flat jaws let the turner reverse the bowl to remove the tenon, and clean up the bottom.

pins that hold it in the flat jaws. Another traditional option is a shop-made jam chuck, which is just a conical block of waste wood mounted in the chuck. The disadvantage of a jam chuck is that the tailstock must be engaged, to provide the pressure that keeps the bowl on the cone. That means that one is always left with a small nub in the center of the bottom that needs to be sanded away. Flat jaws theoretically don't require that the tailstock is engaged, but this author uses it anyway until it absolutely must be removed, because it's in the way (Photo 14). A carbide-tipped detailer makes short work of removing the tenon. Keep in mind that these tools cut along their sides, as well as with the pointed tip.

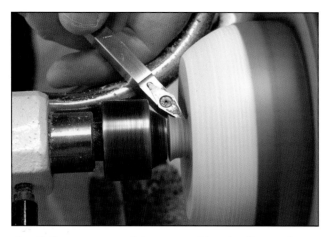

14 Remove most of the tenon with a detailer, again keeping the tailstock engaged for safety.

One word of caution: don't create a narrow V that traps the tool. Keep the V wider than the shape of the cutter.

Sprayed lacquer in disposable cans is a handy way to finish bowls because it dries quickly and is easily sanded if there's a run. It must be sprayed in a designated spray booth or outdoors, for health reasons. A less volatile finish is wipe-on polyurethane. Wax finishes are not durable but, if the bowl will be used to hold food, a mineral oil and beeswax finish works well. This can be purchased pre-mixed in a tub.

Project 3: A Lidded Bowl

On small bowls, two pieces of hardwood can be laminated together after they have been passed across a jointer to render two flat faces. On larger bowls that are too wide for the jointer (this lidded one has a 9" diameter) it's a good idea to mount the hardwood blanks separately on faceplates, true one face of each on the lathe, and then glue them together. The advantage here is that one doesn't have to glue the entire surface, but just a 1" wide rim around the edges. The rest of the front face can be reduced by about 1/16". Use a metal straightedge to check that the matching faces (actually, just the rims) are perfectly flat (Photo 1).

Leave the faceplate in place on one of the laminations. (In this project, the rim is mahogany and the body is 12/4 maple. That, too, could have been laminated, but thick maple isn't difficult to find.) Then spread glue along the 1" wide rim of each lamination and clamp them together. Because a pair of round objects can be awkward to clamp perfectly, it's a good idea to use screws as clamps (Photo 2).

After the glue dries, begin turning by truing the sides of the blank. Here, the sides taper slightly toward the bottom of the bowl, and this is a good opportunity to begin creating that shape. Then move the tool rest to the bottom face, and create the tenon. In this case, because the bowl is so wide, it was decided to leave a small foot around the bottom edge. This gives the completed project more stability, and increases its overall depth. Hollow about 3/8" deep, leaving a roughly 1" wide lip

1 On larger bowls, true one face of each segment on the lathe before gluing them.

2 As the center of the mahogany segment will be removed, screws can be used as clamps.

3 With the glued-up blank trued, create the lip for the foot and the tenon on the bottom.

4 The straight cutter forms the outside of the foot next, still working with the tailstock engaged.

that will later become the foot (Photo 3). This can be done with the square roughing tool. Note that the tailstock is in place for safety, even though the blank is secured to the headstock with a faceplate.

Use a round cutter to shape the concave cut below the rim of the bowl, and a square cutter to create the convex curve that forms most of the outside. Stay with the square cutter to complete the foot (Photo 4). It should be ¼" tall (and it's okay that the tenon is longer).

Reverse the work to gain access to the inside of the bowl (Photo 5). This involves locking the tenon in

5 Reverse the blank (with the tenon now secured in the chuck), and remove the screws.

6 If your live center fits properly, you can leave the faceplate in place and snug up the tailstock.

7 As the recess becomes deeper, replace the metal faceplate with a wooden jam block.

8 Clean up the bottom of the bowl in several light passes taken with the round cutter.

9 True up the rim with a sanding belt stretched on scrap wood, working down the grits.

the chuck. Note that the faceplate remains in place, because on this particular lathe the threaded socket on the faceplate matches up perfectly with the live center in the tailstock. If yours doesn't, simply remove the plate and use the live center alone. The advantage of keeping the faceplate is just that the tailstock is farther away, allowing more room to work.

If you used screws as clamps, now's the time to remove them.

Set the lathe to its lowest speed and begin hollowing the inside of the bowl by creating a groove just inside the glued rims (Photo 6). As soon as this groove penetrates the first lamination, the core will become free. It's trapped by the sidewalls of the bowl, and by the chuck and tailstock front and back, so it may rattle for a second but it won't fly away. Turn off the lathe, slide the tailstock away and then remove the loose core.

A scrap wood jam block can be used to replace the faceplate and core (Photo 7). This allows the turner to keep the tailstock in place for a while

10 A light coat of finish quickly highlights where the surface needs a little more sanding.

11 Cut the simple coves, beads and tenon on the lid with the bottom secured to a faceplate.

longer, while still having good access to the blank. Remove the rest of the waste from the inside of the bowl using a round cutter (Photo 8), and make the final cuts very slowly with a fresh cutter, to achieve a nice, clean finish. Sand the inside and outside surfaces, and use a series of sanding belts backed up by a block of wood to simultaneously sand the entire top rim (Photo 9). Then create a small cove on the inside of the rim for the lid, using a round cutter.

While the bowl is still on the lathe, spray a light coat of sanding sealer all over. This reveals any blemishes that require further sanding, especially in the two areas where the end grain is exposed (Photo 10). Go back down through the grits until these blemishes no longer show up.

The lid is cut to shape, mounted on a faceplate, and then the edges and top are trued up and shaped with the square and round cutters (Photo 11). Dry fit the edge several times so that it conforms to the lip of the bowl. The fit should be loose rather than snug, as wood moves quite a bit with changes in the ambient humidity. Leave a tenon on the top, and then reverse the lid after sanding and mount it in the chuck.

12 Reverse the lid and secure its tenon in the chuck, engage the tailstock, and then hollow it.

Hollow the inside of the lid in the same sequence used for the bowl (Photo 12). Then use flat jaws to hold it while you remove the tenon. Drill a ¼" diameter hole for the knob, and then sand the entire lid down through the grits.

13 The mahogany knob is turned from a chucked blank that has been reduced to a cylinder.

14 The first step is to reduce the end of the cylinder to the diameter of the finished knob.

15 Begin forming the ball by chamfering (putting a 45° angle on) the end of the cylinder.

16 The bottom of the ball begins with a V-cut taken with a square cutter held at an angle.

The knob is a small piece of mahogany turned to a cylinder, and then shaped. Begin by securing a length of mahogany dowel in the chuck (Photo 13). This, of course, can be turned between centers from square stock. Reduce the end of the cylinder to the diameter of the knob (Photo 14). Stay

with the square rougher to chamfer (create a 45 degree corner) on the end of the cylinder (Photo 15). Then begin creating a matching chamfer that will become the bottom of the ball (Photo 16). Remember that the tools cut with their sides as well as their leading edge, so creating a deep

17 Complete the outside curves of the ball by swinging the square cutter in a gentle arc.

18 Move the tool-rest for better support before reducing the top chamfer to a finished curve.

19 Use the square cutter and a light cut to establish the diameter of the base of the knob.

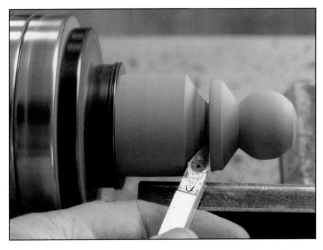

20 A detailer can undercut the bottom of the knob, so the edge fits tightly when installed.

chamfer is relatively easy. Push the tool in slowly (Photo 17), and if it begins to chatter then check that the cutter is flat on the tool rest.

Complete the ball shape on the top of the knob by moving the square cutter in an arc, making sure the end of the handle keeps pace with the cutting edge.

That is, swing the entire tool around in a gentle curving motion (Photo 18). Note that the tool rest is constantly moved to provide adequate support. Next, define the base of the knob by cutting in to your desired diameter (Photo 19). Use a detailer to create a slightly concave cut under the knob (Photo 20), so that when it sits on the curved lid,

21 Use the square cutter to complete the tenon, checking its diameter with a calipers.

22 Sand the knob down through the grits, and then part it from the cylinder with the detailer.

the edges will create a tight visual seal. Leave a small tenon on the bottom, which will be glued into a hole in the lid, to attach the knob. Check the diameter of the tenon with a standard sliding caliper (Photo 21). Finally, slow the lathe to its lowest speed and use the detailer to separate the knob from the cylinder (Photo 22).

Drill a hole in the lid the same diameter as the tenon, and install the knob with glue. Allow the finish to dry fully before placing the lid on the bowl.

CHAPTER 6

Basic Bowl Turning with Concave Cutters

Project 4: Red Oak Undercut Pot

Saucer-shaped (concave) cutters have a mind of their own. They are a lot more difficult to use than flat cutters and perhaps not as versatile. But once mastered, they make superb cuts. A concave cutter can catch more easily in the hands of a novice, or take off in a skid across the surface of the work, but it also can take a beautiful shear cut that leaves a very pleasing finish. These tools are a little less expensive than most flat versions, although the replacement cutters all cost about the same.

This small pot, with its slightly restricted opening, offers an ideal way to explain how concave cutters work. Begin by mounting a blank to a faceplate, and engage the tailstock with a live center (Photo 1) for support. The blank shown here is two 6/4 thicknesses of kiln dried, plainsawn red oak that have been face glued. The grain runs the same direction in both. (To learn more about buying wood, see Chapter 10.)

Set the lathe at a speed of about 800 to 1,000 RPM, but don't turn it on yet.

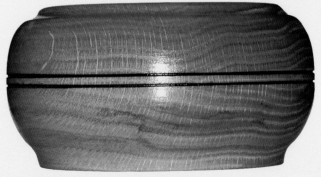

1 The grains in glued-up blanks should line up, or the layers might separate as they move.

HUNTER TOOLS

2 Hunter Tools' #4 lathe chisel has a saucer-shaped insert on a round steel shaft.

3 Depending on how tall you are, set the tool-rest height so that the bevel rubs the wood.

4 Rotate the tool until the cutter is at about 10 o'clock. It's still not contacting the wood.

The tool shown here with the saucer-shaped cutter is a Hunter #4 (Photo 2), which has a ½" diameter insert that has a slight bevel to its outside (that is, it tapers from the top down). Keep in mind that this tool is *never* used flat! If it is fed into the spinning work flat (where the screw head is facing the ceiling), it will most definitely catch. It was designed for use at an angle.

Begin deciding on the height of the tool rest by looking at the bevel of the tool. That's the area of the shaft that lies directly below the cutter. Note how it slopes a little toward the bottom. Before the lathe is turned on, the tool rest is set a little below

center, so that this bevel rubs the wood (Photo 3). Move the rest in fairly close, too, so that it supports the tool and leaves a small gap between the rest and the wood. Manually rotate the work to make sure it turns freely and safely.

The next paragraph is written for right-handed turners, but the same technique applies in reverse to left-handed turning.

Place the tool on the rest (still not turned on) and rotate the shaft so that the top of the cutter is facing halfway between the ceiling and the wall to your right (Photo 4). Swing the handle to your left, past

5 In this view from directly on top of the cutter, the handle is being swung to the right.

6 As the handle swings around, the cutter makes contact. Control the swing to control the cut.

7 Form the foot (the rim upon which the pot will stand) and the tenon on the bottom.

90 degrees, so that the bevel on the bottom of the tool is parallel to the wood (Photo 5). Turn on the lathe and gently ease the tool in until the bevel makes contact. The tool is not yet cutting. Slowly swing the end of the handle to the right until the cutter contacts the wood and begins making shavings (Photo 6). The more you swing, the deeper the cut. The more open the cutter is (that is, the more it is tilted so that the top of it faces the ceiling more than the wall to your right), the more aggressively it will cut. Keep in mind when you start that the blank isn't true (perfectly round) yet, so there will be a little bit of chatter as the cutter makes contact with a high spot, then passes freely over a low spot, and then hits the next high spot. When the blank is true, increase the speed. Hunter Tools recommend 1800 to 2200 RPM.

Shape the outside of the pot so that it curves gently from top to bottom. Rotate the tool to close the cutter (more vertical than horizontal) for finer, cleaner finishing cuts. Note that the side of the pot curves both at the top and bottom. The top curve reduces the opening (neck), making this a pot rather than a bowl. If it reduced the opening even more, it would be called a vessel.

Remove the tailstock when the outside is shaped, and create a foot and a tenon on the bottom (Photo 7). The foot will allow the completed pot to sit on a surface with minimal contact, making it more stable. The tenon is to hold the blank in a chuck while the inside is hollowed. If necessary, use a square roughing tool or even a traditional skew to square up the sides of the tenon. It should be about 5/16" to 3/8" long.

Reverse the pot and secure the tenon in the chuck. Make sure it is seated properly, doesn't bottom out, and the shoulders are snugly against the jaws. Then begin hollowing by drilling out much of the waste

8 Secure the tenon in a chuck and drill out the center with a Forstner bit, to save some time.

9 One can work from the center out, or from the rim in, as Hunter tools cut in either direction.

10 Stay with the #4 tool to remove most of the waste, leaving the top of the walls thicker.

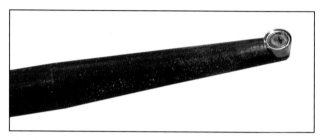

11 Switch to a smaller #1 tool to make final passes on the bottom and halfway up the sidewalls.

12 The #1 C tool works wonderfully to clean up the walls below the pot's shoulder.

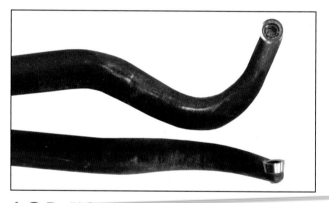

13 The #1 C tool is a swan neck with a cutter installed flat, and it can be a little aggressive.

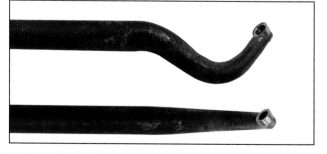

14 The #1 Shoulder tool's cutter is installed at an angle and it works right up under the shoulder.

15 The heavy Hunter #3 Hercules tool is ideal for making silky smooth final cuts on the inside.

16 The #3 Hercules also works well to blend the outside curves of the pot into each other.

with a Forstner bit (Photo 8), with the lathe at its lowest speed. Yes, the purists are mumbling, but drilling takes a whole lot less time, and it's safer, too. Be aware that Forstner bits have a point on them, and this must penetrate no farther than the inside bottom of the pot.

Carbide cutters let turners rethink a lot of the traditional rules. When hollowing, one can rotate the tool in either direction so it cuts out from the center, or in from the edges. Begin enlarging the hole using a Hunter #4 (Photo 9), keeping in mind that the cutter face must never be fully open (flat), or it will catch. This tool will remove most of the material along the walls (Photo 10). Switch to the similar but smaller #1 (Photo 11) to clean up the cut along the bottom and lower walls.

Hunter's swan neck tools do a nice job of cleaning up the rest of the sidewalls, and hollowing out closer to the neck. The #1 C tool (Photo 12, 13) is a mild swan neck that works from the bottom of the wall until it begins to curve in toward the opening. The #1 Shoulder Tool (Photo 14) works best close up under the shoulder, as the angle of the cutter slopes downward, so it isn't so aggressive. When it comes to swan necks, grain direction plays a role in hollowing, even with carbide inserts. With

that in mind, here are Hunter Tools' instructions on using their swan neck tools for this process:

"For the underside of box rims, cut from the rim to the major diameter of the body of the box. Once you reach that diameter, lift the tool and cut from the bottom upward to the major diameter of the body of the box." What they're saying is that the swan neck tools work best when the cut begins either at the top or bottom of the inside curve, and finishes at the middle.

To flatten the inside bottom of the pot and to complete the transition from bottom to sidewalls, the Hunter #3 Hercules tool is a good choice (Photo 15). This heavy, square-shafted tool has the saucer-shaped cutter mounted at a downward angle. It can be used to cut down the walls toward the corner, and then come out from the center toward the corner, and it delivers a very smooth cut with little risk of chatter or catching. It can also be used to deliver a smooth finish on the outside curves of the pot (Photo 16).

It's a good idea to sand and finish all of the pot except the bottom at this time, while it's still secured in the chuck. To disguise the joint between the two blocks of wood that made up the original

17 The bumpers on flat jaws can mar the work, so it's a good idea to stick masking tape on them.

18 Being rotated slowly as the diameter changes, Hunter's #4 tool will remove the tenon.

19 Stay with the flat jaws and a portable drill mounted sander to clean up the bottom.

20 Spray finishes at the lowest speed, or runs will feather out into concentric rivulets.

blank, a couple of lines can be burned in with a wire. One of these rests precisely on the joint, and the other is about ⅜" above it.

After burning, turn the speed all the way up for sanding, and then down to about 1200 RPM for spraying on a quick-drying clear lacquer.

Flat jaws are a great way to secure a bowl or pot by its opening, so that the bottom can be cleaned up. Despite the softness of their rubber bumpers, they can still slightly mar a sanded surface, so it's a good idea to put a single layer of blue painter's masking tape on the bumpers before installing the work (Photo 17). Once secure, set the speed at about 1500 RPM and use the #4 tool to remove the tenon (Photo 18). Sand the bottom next (Photo 19), and then apply the finish (Photo 20).

Hunter carbide inserts and all of the other saucer-shaped cutters seem to require a lot more practice that flat-topped carbide cutters. They are a little bit more affordable, and some seasoned turners who have spent many years "riding the bevel" will perhaps find them more comfortable than the less complicated flat versions. These convex cutters, with practice, can deliver a very smooth surface, but they also seem more apt to catch and skid than their flat cousins do. They are not really hogs, so drilling out the core or using a flat rougher to remove much of the waste is still a viable option. One big advantage to them seems to be that they slice end grain rather than scraping it. Anyone who makes bowls knows that the two areas of end grain on a bowl are the most difficult to clean up, and with these tools that problem virtually disappears.

CHAPTER 7

Simple Hollow Vessels

Project 5: Cross-grain Oak Vase

Hollow vessels have always been the ultimate challenge in turning. From a strictly technical viewpoint (that is, ignoring aesthetics), bragging rights go to the turner who can make the largest vessel with the smallest opening, and some artists will spend days on a single piece. There are numerous deep hollowing systems on the market. Most of them are built around a jig that holds a very long handled chisel parallel to the floor, so that the turner only has to deal with the X-Y axis. The Z-axis (up and down) is simply eliminated. The newer hollowing systems also incorporate lasers, so that one can instantly tell how thin the walls of the vessel are, and where the cutter is located. A sensible suggestion here might be to turn several vessels without those very expensive jigs before investing in one. That way, you'll know what questions to ask.

Hollowing the inside of a vessel with flat-topped carbide cutters got a lot easier in late 2011, when Easy Wood Tools introduced their new Easy Hollower package. This is a progressive system that uses three tools in sequence to remove the waste. It begins with an almost straight #1 Hollower that cleans the bottom of the void and begins to work up

1 Following the pattern, use the square tool to create the outside curves on a glued-up blank.

2 With the work still on the faceplate, inside curves can be completed with a round cutter.

the sidewalls. Next, the #2 Hollower, a soft radius swan neck tool, works on the tops of the sidewalls. The last tool, the #3, is a hard radius swan neck that cleans out under the shoulder. The smaller the opening, the smaller diameter vessel these tools can create. That's because the shafts are flat and very wide above the swan neck, and the curved, thin part of the shaft isn't very long. The projects shown here each have an opening sized to allow the tools to work well.

There are two vases here. One has grain running across it, and the other has the grain running along its length. That delivers two very different looking vases with similar profiles. Cutting across the grain (the first vase) is similar to turning a bowl. Cutting along the grain is essentially the same as turning between centers (spindle cutting).

For the first vase, the process begins with creating a blank by gluing ten squares together (each 1" x 4½" x 4½"), with their grain running in the same direction. When the glue dries, band saw the block to create a cylinder. Attach a faceplate to one end using 1¾" sheetmetal screws driven into pre-drilled pilot holes. The thick sacrificial base helps to give the project mass, and the long screws are necessary

because the vessel is relatively tall and it needs a good anchor.

Mount the cylinder between centers and reduce it to 4⁷⁄₁₆" diameter, keeping the tailstock in place for stability and running at very low speed. Begin shaping the outside of the vessel using the square rougher (Photo 1), and the round finisher (Photo 2). Here, the speed can be increased to about 1200 RPM. The suggested shape is shown on the full-size pattern (right), but don't be overly concerned if it varies a bit. As with all patterns, it's a good idea to photocopy it, glue it to some ¼" plywood, and cut it in relief (that is, throw away the vase and keep its outline). Then the lathe can be stopped at any time, and the negative pattern can be used to check progress simply by holding it against the blank.

Sand the outside down through the grits (80, 150, 220, 280) with the lathe running at least 2500 RPM, and then slow it down to its lowest speed. At this point, many turners like to finish the outside with sprayed lacquer, applied in several very light coats. Sand between coats with 400-grit paper.

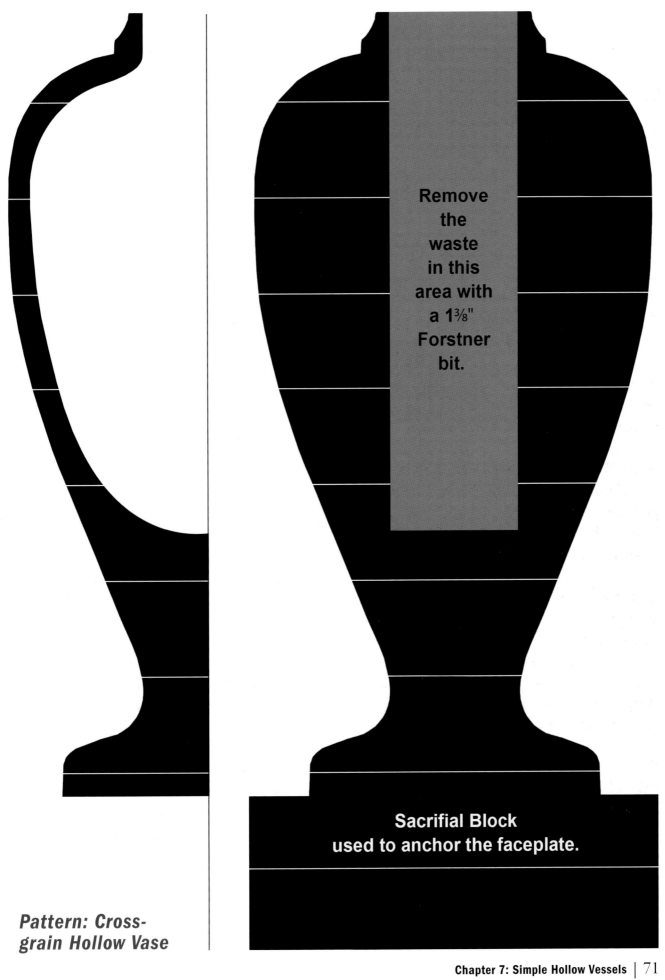

Remove
the
waste
in this
area with
a 1⅜"
Forstner
bit.

Sacrifial Block
used to anchor the faceplate.

Pattern: Cross-grain Hollow Vase

3 Drill out the core with a Forstner bit the diameter of the neck opening you wish to create.

4 Deep hollowing is a lot easier with two tool-rests. One needs to buy an extra banjo for this.

5 To dramatically reduce chatter, press firmly with your thumb between the two tool-rests.

6 When the straight tool has removed all it can, switch to a swan neck for the shoulders.

With a 1⅜" Forstner bit secured in a lathe-mounted drill chuck (Photo 3), slowly remove the core. Drilling cuts down on the amount of hollowing to be done with chisels, so it's a big timesaver. Many hardware stores and Web sites sell inexpensive extensions for Forstner bits, letting a turner drill deeper holes than the original bit's shaft will allow.

When the drilling is done, speed up to about 1500 RPM to begin hollowing. The long reach of the #1 Hollower (Photo 4) will remove most of the waste. Reaching this deep can be quite intimidating with traditional tools, but the flat bottom of the tool's shaft lends it a great deal of stability. And to virtually

eliminate any chance of a catch, more and more turners are investing in a second banjo (the base for the tool rest), and using two tool-rests, one behind the other. The idea here is to use one's thumb to apply lots of pressure between the rests (Photo 5). Used banjos can often be found on eBay™ and Craigslist™, and new ones aren't very expensive for mini and midi lathes. The secure feeling one gets from the two-rest method is well worth the investment.

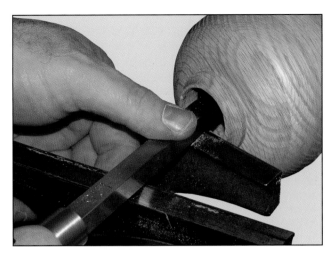

7 Move slowly when easing the straight hollower (shown) and the swan necks into the sidewalls.

8 A shop-built (shown) or a commercial bowl steady rest adds a large degree of safety here.

When switching to the #2 and eventually the #3 Hollowers, guide the swan necks gently into the opening (Photo 6) and leave the two tool-rests in place. Very gently swivel the rear of the tool handle to the right (Photo 7), until contact is made. These tools seem to prefer to make contact and then be pulled toward the opening, rather than starting near the neck and be pushed toward the base. Constantly check the thickness of the walls, using a large turner's calipers.

A bowl steady rest (commercially available from retailers such as Oneway Manufacturing and All In One Wood Tools) is a real boon when hollowing vessels. The one shown here was shop-built (Photo 8). It consists of a plywood circle with three in-line skate wheels that are mounted on short lengths of stock, and then these are simply clamped to the circle about 120 degrees apart. They ride on the widest part of the vessel (Photo 9). The steady rest virtually eliminates vibration, and it hopefully will

9 Steady rests work best near the neck, where the wheels can ride the widest diameter.

catch a loose turning before it becomes airborne. Plans for a similar one are available online at newwoodworker.com/stdyrstpln.html.

To remove the tenon on either this piece or the long-grain vessel described next, skip to the final paragraph in this chapter.

Project 6: Long-grain Ash Vase

With this second vase, the tool is cutting along the grain. In this orientation, the integrity of the blank is a consideration no matter what kind of tools are being used (carbide or traditional). As the grain runs the length of the work-piece, the ends are now both revealing exposed end-grain. Think about chopping firewood. One swings the axe head into the end-grain to take advantage of nature and to allow the split to follow the grain. When a turning blank is between centers, there is a sharp spur in one end and a pointed live center in the other (Photo 1), and the lathe applies pressure to both as the tailstock is locked. Keys here are to allow a glued-up blank to dry thoroughly in the clamps (at least overnight) so the glue fully cures, and to check and double-check a one-piece blank for any signs of cracks, fissures, checking or other defects that could possibly give way under pressure.

As with any turning between centers, the grain runs left to right (parallel to the bed of the lathe), so there's a chance that the tool will peel away more than the turner intends. That is, the cut may follow the grain, so one can't be too aggressive here.

Begin this project by reducing a 4½" x 4½" x 11" ash, kiln-dried, glued-up blank to a cylinder (Photo 2). This is done with a large square rougher, with the lathe running at its slowest speed. Note that the chips here are generally longer than the cutter is wide, because of the grain direction. Be aware that, as you knock off the corners, large chips will go airborne, so using a face shield is imperative. They run $20 to $30 at most hardware stores. When the blank is round, turn up the speed (1200 to 1500 RPM).

Following the full-size pattern, stay with the rougher to begin removing waste in the area that

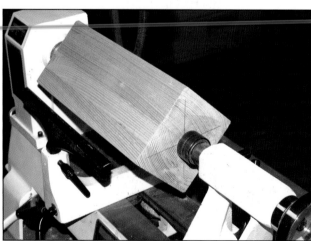

1 Long-grain vessels can begin with a glued-up blank (shown) or a solid piece of stock.

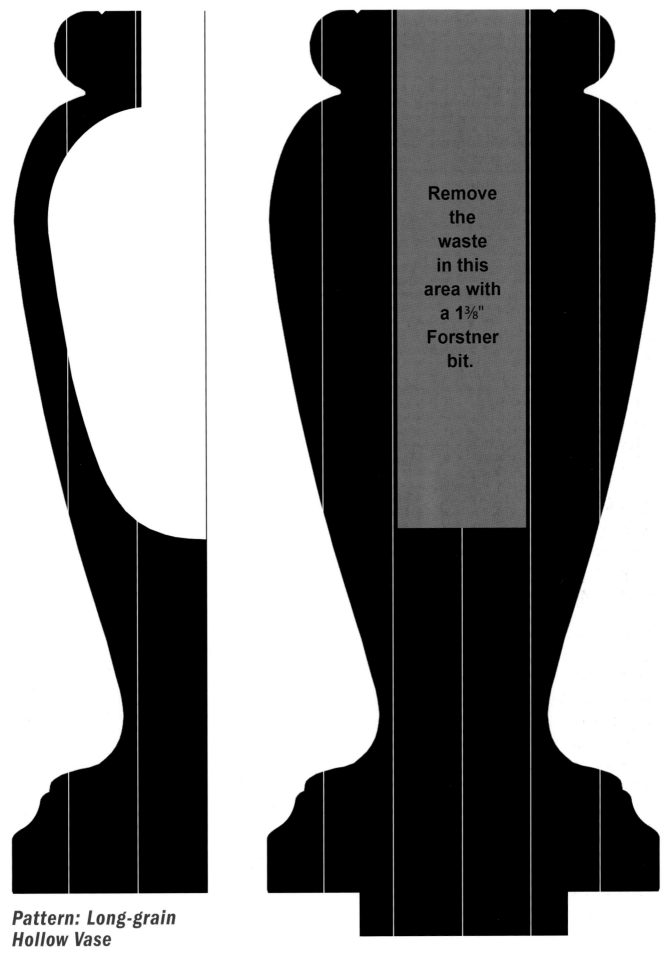

Remove the waste in this area with a 1⅜" Forstner bit.

Pattern: Long-grain Hollow Vase

2 The first step is to reduce the blank to the largest possible cylinder with a square cutter.

3 With the work between a drive center (spur) and a live center, begin by shaping the base.

4 The bottom of the vase tapers up from a fairly narrow cove just above the base.

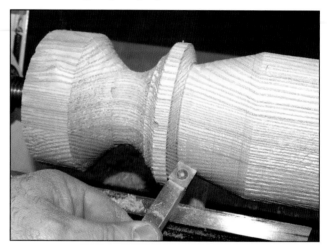

5 A square rougher makes quick work of creating the long taper that ends at the cove.

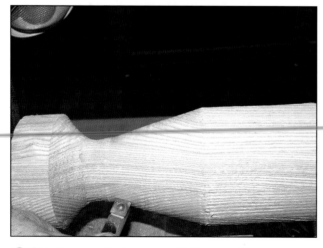

6 Sidegrain can be hairy, so a light pass with a new, sharp cutter will clean up the taper.

7 Stay with the square cutter to create a tenon on the bottom of the base, sized to fit your chuck.

8 The cove, made with a sharp, round cutter, is about half the thickness of the base.

9 A small, decorative rabbet completes the coves, and this is cut with a square carbide insert.

separates the foot from the body (the narrowest part of the finished vase). This cut will remove waste a lot faster if it is taken at about 45° (Photo 3). Switch to a large round finisher to reduce the area to a gentle curve (Photo 4).

Go back to the square rougher to meld the sides of the vase into a seamless transition from the widest diameter to the narrowest (Photo 5). By taking about ⅛" wide cuts at a time, the rougher will quickly remove all of this waste (Photo 6). Stay with the same tool to create the tenon on the bottom of the vase (Photo 7). As always, this should be just a little larger than the diameter of your chuck when the jaws have been adjusted to the point where they are closest to creating a perfect circle. With most chucks, this will be when

they are almost but not fully closed. The closer they are to a circle, the more of each jaw is in direct contact with the tenon. Remember that the tenon can't bottom out (that is, it can't be too long). The shoulders *must* be in full contact with the chuck.

This vase has a large solid base, so a cove and rabbet are used to visually lighten its look. The cove is cut with the round finisher (Photo 8), sweeping very slightly from side to side to create an arc that is a little larger than the diameter of the cutter. In red oak and similar wide grained species (ash, butternut etc.), a very gentle touch with a new, very sharp insert does a wonderful job of cleaning up the surface, especially on side grain. Create the rabbet, which is just a simple step, using the corner of the large square rougher (Photo 9).

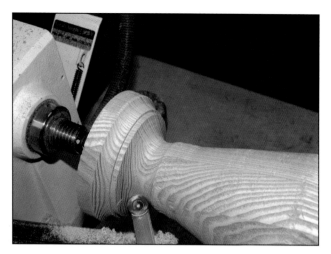

10 Stay with the sharp round cutter to clean up the surface and blend the base into the taper.

11 For a very smooth finish, use a brand new cutter and move the tool as slowly as possible.

12 The large square cutter makes the outside curves at the top of the taper and on the shoulder.

That sharp new cutter in the finisher also works well to clean up the transition from the base to the body (Photo 10). The difference in surface quality between rough and finish passes is immediately obvious. By moving the cutter very slowly across the surface, you can blend and gently shape at the same time (Photo 11).

Before forming the sidewalls of the vase, unplug the lathe and switch from the drive center (spur) to a chuck. If you wait until the entire body is formed to switch over, the vase will never lie in the exact same plane as it was, so the orbit will be a little eccentric. That is, when the blank is locked in a chuck, it will

be a little off-center and you will have to re-turn the outside to make it true again. It's best to switch over early.

Return to the square rougher (still at about 1200-1500 RPM) to create the curve at the shoulders of the vase (Photo 12). As the tool moves toward the center of a long-grain turning, more and more end-grain is being exposed. With traditional tools, this would have been an issue that required changing direction and using different parts of the ground edge of a gouge, but here, all that is required is patience. Move slowly, keeping the tool parallel to the floor, and swing the back end around as you describe the arc. That is, the shaft of the tool should be at 90° to the wood surface, and as the tool travels around the arc toward the center of the blank, the back end of the handle needs to move rather quickly to the right, to allow the cutting edge to maintain this angle.

Complete the curve using a detailer (the tool with the diamond-shaped cutter). The point of the detailer defines a groove between the shoulders and the wide lip of the vase (Photo 13). It's important that deep grooves like this are made just slightly wider than the cutter, so the tip doesn't become

13 Refine the groove between the shoulder and the neck of the vessel using a detailer.

14 One can also use the sides of the detailer to clean up any "hairy" grain on the arc of the lip.

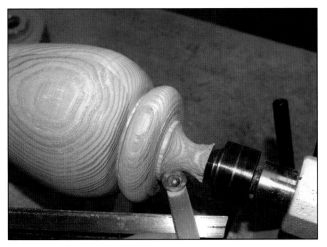

15 Remove most of the waste above the neck with a round cutter, with the tailstock in place.

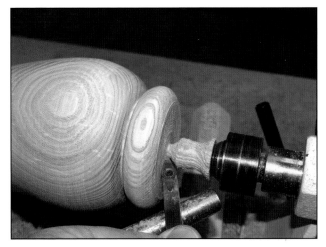

16 Switch to the detailer to reduce the last of the wasteto almost nothing, and flatten the top.

trapped, and catch. The sides of the detailer are sharp, so it's a great tool for cleaning up any "hairy" grain on the shoulder, and also for forming the top arc of the lip (Photo 14).

Use the large round finisher to remove most of the waste above the lip (Photo 15), and reduce the last of it with the detailer (Photo 16). Turn off the lathe, slide the tailstock out of the way, and simply snap off the last of the waste (Photo 17). Bring the tailstock back to the work and secure it. Any time you can work with the tailstock in place, it's a good idea to do so. It's a lot safer to have the work secured by two devices than one.

17 When the waste is down to about ⅛", stop the lathe, retard the tailstock, and break it off.

Turn the speed up to about 2500 RPM, and thoroughly sand the entire outside of the vase. Work down from 60-grit to 80, 120, 180, 220 and 280 (Photo 18). Skipping grits will really show scratches on a long-grain turning, as the abrasive (sandpaper) is cutting across the grain. When

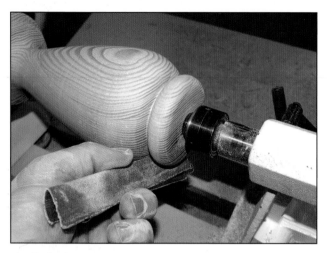

18 Re-engage the tailstock, increase the speed, and sand the outside down through the grits.

sanding, double the paper to reduce the chance of it getting too hot to hold.

There are three good reasons to sand from the bottom of the work. If the wood grabs the paper, it will safely slip out of your fingers. Next, the sanding residue (dust) travels away from the operator when the paper is held below the work. And finally, with your hand and the paper out of the way, you can watch the progress on the top surface of the turning wood.

When the vase is sanded, turn off the lathe. Replace the live center in the tailstock with a drill chuck, and reduce the lathe speed to its slowest option (usually about 500 RPM). Secure a 1⅜" Forstner bit (35mm works, too) in the chuck and drill in as far as the shaft will allow (Photo 19), without bottoming out.

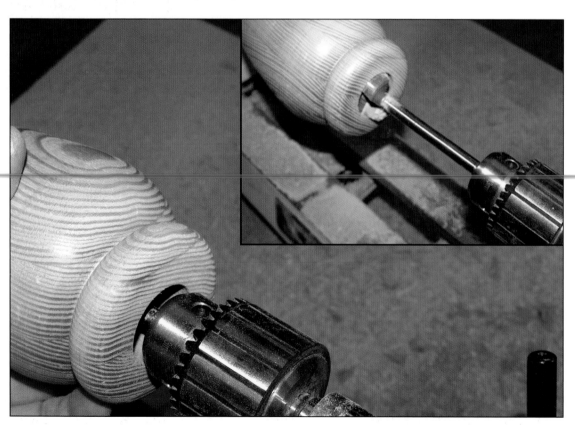

19 Use a long Forstner bit (or a short one with a shaft extension), to drill out the vase's core.

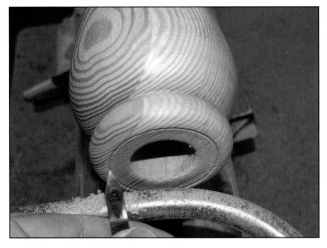

20 A decorative groove cut with the detailer is a simple way to dress up the top of the vase.

21 Quick-drying lacquer can be applied to the outside of the vase in several light coats.

22 Sand between coats of finish with 400-grit wet or dry paper, building to a deep, rich surface.

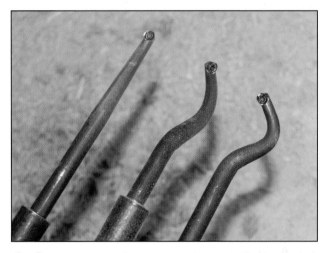

23 According to the company, Hunter hollowing tools work best at 1800-2200 RPM.

The neck can be decorated with a thin groove cut with the detailer (Photo 20), and then the top should be sanded before a finish is applied (Photo 21). Spraying several thin coats of lacquer while the lathe turns at its slowest speed gives ash a rich, deep appearance (Photo 22).

At this point, the vase is hollow enough to hold items such as dried flowers, and one could stop here. However, opening up the inside of the vase is a very satisfying process. This time, saucer-shaped cutters from Hunter Tools were used (Photo 23). Here's how the company describes the process:

"The Hunter Tools are best used at higher RPM (1800-2200 RPM) to have sufficient surface speed. With fine tool control you can peel off shavings that are onionskin thin. The surface will be so smooth that little sanding will be needed. Of course as with any other cutting tool you will be cutting with the grain for the smoothest cut. So for the underside of box rims, cut from the rim to the major diameter of the body of the box (Photo 24). Once you reach that diameter, lift the tool and cut from the bottom upward to the major diameter of the body of the box. It is mesmerizing to peel these ultrafine shavings so be careful or you may make the inside merge with the outside.

24 To avoid catches, the straight section of this tool's shaft should have been on the tool-rest.

25 Hunter's #1 Taper Tools, designed for small boxes, were used to great effect in the vase.

26 The hollowing tools are short, so a Hunter #4 was used to go beyond their reach.

"There is a learning curve with the Hunter. You have to learn to rotate the tool clockwise into the cut with the tool slightly above center and angled downward somewhat like a scraper. The tool does not scrape; it cuts like nothing you have ever seen. Don't expect to hog out the interior of a box or something similar quickly. The tool is not designed for that. It is a final form and finish cut tool."

Here, the three #1 Taper Tools, originally designed for small boxes, were used to great effect in the vase (Photo 25). With the core drilled out, they work in bigger projects than those for which they were designed. Again, here is the company's take on them:

"Designed by Mark St. Leger, noted box maker, (these tools) are to be used on vessel's 3" tall max and smaller. These tools can be used to rough out hollow forms, but the best use is for finishing and final form shaping. The #1 Straight Tool will clean up the bottom, the # 1 Hook Tool will clean up the sides, and then the hardest cut for any turner is to clean up the shoulder, which the #1 Shoulder or Back Tool is designed to reach."

These short shafted hollowing tools won't quite reach down to the bottom of the 4" deep cavity, so a Hunter #4 was used to clean up the bottom of the void (Photo 26). It also cleaned up most of the sidewalls (Photo 27), reaching high enough so the swan neck tools could take over. Remember to slide the straight tool into the opening so the cutter is vertical (the top is facing left), touch the wood, and then very slowly rotate it clockwise until it begins to cut. The set of three box making tools have very small cutters, so the propensity of these saucer-shaped tools to catch is greatly reduced. The swan necks can be fed into the opening almost flat (Photo 28), because the cutters are already mounted at an angle.

27 Straight tools clean up most of the sidewalls until the swan neck tools can take over.

28 Swan necks can be fed into an opening flat, because the cutters are mounted at an angle.

The fact that this vase has no end-grain on the sidewalls reduces resistance, but there's a trade-off. The cut feels safer, but it isn't as clean. Hollowing in kiln-dried, long-grain applications, the cut is not as smooth as it is in end-grain boxes (for which they were designed), but nevertheless the tools feel very safe and they certainly remove a lot of waste rather quickly.

When the inside is hollowed, it's tempting to keep the lathe running and insert a couple of fingers with sandpaper to clean up the inside. This is an absolute no-no. The vessel will grab your fingers and break them. One can roll up a sheet of sandpaper and insert it into the neck to clean up just that area, holding onto the part of it that extends beyond the opening with a light grip.

In the Tips section on their Web site, the East Texas Woodturners' Association (easttexaswoodturners. org) has published a tip on how to build a sander for exactly this purpose. It was originally conceived by an old friend, Wyoming woodturner Ellis Hein, and is a wonderful finger saver.

Removing Tenons

With the vase fashioned, hollowed and the outside finished, it's time to remove the tenon on the bottom. There are several ways to do this. One of the most obvious is to just hold the piece against a belt or disk sander, but the problem with that method is that it rarely results in a perfectly flat bottom. We tend to tip things a little to one side.

A second way is to band saw it off, and then touch up with a sander. Again, the problem is holding the work-piece at 90° to the band saw table. One could build a sled with scrap wood that supports and raises the narrower parts of the vase so they're horizontal, but the next vessel off the lathe will require a different set of supports, as no two turnings are ever identical.

The easiest way to remove the tenon is to chuck the work back on the lathe, securing it by the neck in "Jumbo", or flat jaws (Photo 29). Note that the tailstock has been engaged, because it always should be, whenever possible. With the lathe running slow (about 800 RPM), use a round finisher to remove most of the tenon (Photo 30). The slow speed will deliver a somewhat rough cut, but flat jaws are notoriously unreliable and running

29 When the vase is hollow, mount it in flat jaws (with the tailstock engaged) to remove the tenon.

30 Set the tool-rest so it supports a round cutter and use this to remove most of the tenon.

31 Reduce the waste with a detailer, then turn off the lathe and snap off the last bit of waste.

32 Clean up the bottom working down the grits, using a disc sander chucked in a portable drill.

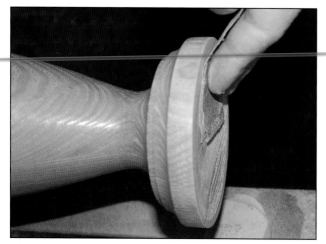

33 Hand sand with the grain for a clean, professional-looking finish on the bottom of the vase.

them at high speed just doesn't seem like a great idea, even with the tailstock engaged. Remove the last of the waste with a detailer (Photo 31), and then back off the tailstock. Sand the base with a small rotary disc chucked in a portable drill (Photo 32), completing the job with several grits of hand-held sandpaper (Photo 33). Apply several light coats of sprayed lacquer, and your long-grain ash vase is good to go.

CHAPTER 8

Compound Hollow Vessels

Project 7: Mahogany and Maple Urn

Hollowing out deep vessels can be a tricky task that requires a fair amount of experience, and also some special tools. The traditional method is to harvest a length of tree trunk and rough turn it while it's still green, then coat it in wax and let it dry (one year for every inch of thickness). After that, long gouges are used to laboriously remove waste from the inside. These tools reach a long way past the tool rest, and can be especially susceptible to catches in the hands of the inexperienced.

The method described here uses kiln dried hardwood, so it is ideally suited to carbide insert tools. Dry lumber eliminates the rough turning process, the waxing, and also the long wait for air-drying. And because the orb is turned in two parts (hence, "compound") and then joined together, the entire process is no trickier than basic bowl turning. It also allows the turner to apply a good finish to the interior, which can be difficult to do in a simple (one-piece) hollow vessel.

The project requires two 4" diameter faceplates, a drill chuck for the lathe, a circle cutter (or a 5" diameter hole saw or a jigsaw), and a four-jaw chuck.

1 Both halves of the orb can be glued up at the same time, after drilling two holes.

2 A compass is used to draw a circle that describes the largest outside diameter of the orb.

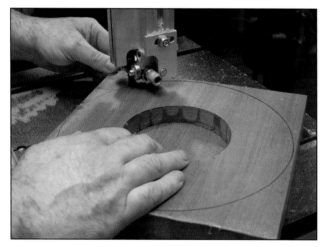

3 The two halves are separated and then individually band sawn to their rough shape.

4 The cut-out from one face of the blank is glued to the other, to increase the orb's volume.

Start with a wide, flat board that is at least 48" long. Shown here is ⁵⁄₄ mahogany that was 1⅛" thick and 10½" wide. Walnut would be another good choice. The critical constraint is that the board is flat and parallel, so it needs to be face jointed and then run through a planer. Crosscut it into two 24" long boards.

Remove the twist drill (the pilot bit) from a 5" diameter hole saw and drill one hole in each board. These are centered 5¼" from one end and the same distance from each edge. This is a drill press operation, with the board clamped in place. It is unsafe to do with a portable drill. An alternative here is to use a scroll saw or jigsaw with a small starter hole, because you need to save the waste intact.

Face glue and clamp the boards together, making sure the holes don't line up (Photo 1). Eighteen spring clamps provide plenty of pressure for this. After the glue dries, use a compass to draw two circles. Each of these is centered in one of the 5" voids and it needs to describe the largest circle that the board will accommodate (Photo 2). These two large circles must be the same size.

Band saw each large circle from the board (Photo 3). Then turn it over with the void facing down and

5 With the blank mounted on a faceplate, hollow the inside. Note the tailstock jam block.

6 A square rougher is used to flatten and clean the bottom of the lower half of the orb.

glue on the waste from the 5" hole (Photo 4). A long-reach clamp helps a lot here, and measuring in from the edge at several locations helps gets the cap relatively centered.

Center a 4" faceplate in the 5" hole in one of your two blanks, and attach it with screws. This first blank will be the bottom half of the orb (the base, as opposed to the lid). Mount the base on the lathe, snug up the tailstock with a live center in place, and set the speed for about 800 RPM. Turn the outside profile (see drawing, p. 88) using a carbide-tipped rougher. You're just after the general shape now, as you'll refine, sand and finish it later.

When the exterior profile has been established, remove the faceplate and remount it on the 5" diameter cap that you glued to the outside of the base. On my favorite midi lathe (a JET 1220), the quill in the tailstock is not very long, and its foot tends to limit where I can place the tool rest. So, I move the tailstock back a couple of inches and use one of several small turned cylinders (called a jam block) to bridge the gap and keep pressure on the bowl (Photo 5). The faceplate mounted on the headstock would probably be enough to secure

7 With the work spinning slowly on the lathe, a disc sander in a portable drill sands the inside.

the work, but there's a nice feeling of security in using the tailstock too, when it's available.

Use the square rougher to remove most of the waste from inside the blank, and then remove the jam block to complete the task. The walls should be about ⅜" thick, and flare out to ¾" for the lip around the opening, to provide a larger gluing surface. Use the rougher to flatten the bottom (Photo 6). A small, round, sponge-backed sander in a drill, widely available from turning tool suppliers, makes quick work of sanding the inside of any bowl (Photo 7). Run down through the grits from 80 through 120, 150 and 220.

8 The undercut rim (widest at the lip) is evened out with a sanding belt stretched on wood.

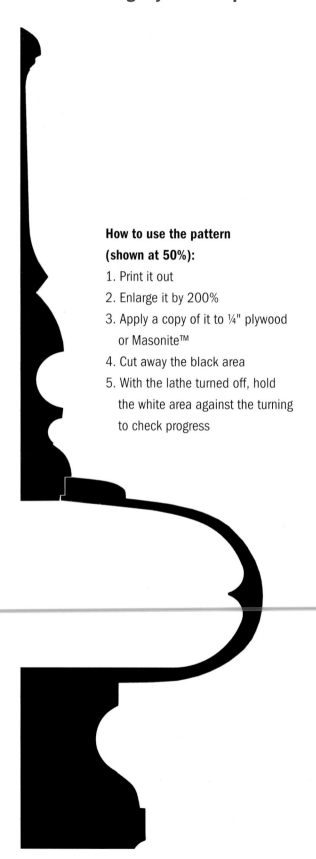

9 Finish is applied to the inside now, as it will be impossible once the orb has been assembled.

As the two halves of the orb need to mate properly, their outer lips must be absolutely flat. A 40-grit sanding belt stretched on a block of wood works like a platen: when it bridges the opening in the bowl, it delivers a flat and true surface (Photo 8). Be careful to rest both ends of the belt on the lip, and keep it moving slightly or it will dig grooves in the wood.

Finish the inside of the blank with a spray lacquer while the part is still turning on the lathe (Photo 9). Several light coats work best. The revolving motion helps avert runs, and it also helps the lacquer dry to the touch in minutes. Avoid spraying finish on the

Pattern: Mahogany and Maple Urn

How to use the pattern (shown at 50%):
1. Print it out
2. Enlarge it by 200%
3. Apply a copy of it to ¼" plywood or Masonite™
4. Cut away the black area
5. With the lathe turned off, hold the white area against the turning to check progress

10 The rim is finish sanded to remove any lacquer and provide a good gluing surface.

11 With a faceplate attached to the inside, the outside of the lid of the orb can be turned.

lip, as this will be glued. After the finish dries, dress the lip again with a 120-grit sanding belt backed up by a piece of wood (Photo 10). This removes any lacquer on the lip, which will ensure a better bond when the two halves are eventually glued together. Leave the faceplate in place for now.

The Lid

Screw the second faceplate to the inside of the lid blank, centering it in the 5" diameter opening. Then rough turn the outside profile (Photo 11). The dimension at the lip needs to be as close as possible to the outside dimension of the base.

Create a tenon on the end that is slightly larger in diameter than the opening that your four-jaw chuck makes when the jaws create a perfect circle. The tenon should be long enough so that the shoulders sit snug on the chuck when the end of the tenon is still 1/16" shy of bottoming out inside the chuck.

To hollow the inside of the lid, remove the blank and reverse it to mount it in the chuck. Bring up the tailstock, extend the quill, and then secure the blank with a jam block (Photo 12). Follow the same process used in the base, removing the waste using a square rougher and then a round finishing

12 Repeat the process from the base, using a jam block to keep the tailstock engaged for safety.

tool. Flatten the bottom, sand and lacquer the inside, and then flatten the lip. Leave the lid in the chuck, and the chuck on the lathe, and now you're ready to make an orb.

Glue Up

One of the most wonderful features of a lathe is that is can be used as a clamp to glue the two halves of the orb together. To do so, begin by unplugging the lathe. Next, check that the opening in the faceplate (the one that is still attached to the base) will fit on the live center in your tailstock. The live center is usually conical (cone-shaped), and as the

13 The cone on most live centers will fit perfectly in the opening of a 1"-8 TPI faceplate.

14 Using the lathe as a clamp, the halves are glued together, lined up, and have pressure applied.

15 Crank the tailstock enough to achieve a nice, tight seal all the way around, but not too tight.

16 When dry, dress the joint with a square carbide cutter and the glue line will virtually disappear.

opening in the faceplate is round and of a slightly smaller diameter, it should be able to just sit on the live center when it's under slight pressure (Photo 13). If it doesn't, use a small scrap of wood between the live center and the faceplate.

Lay some paper towels on the lathe bed to catch any excess glue and then apply a liberal coat of glue to the lip on the base. Line up the two halves and slide the tailstock forward so that the assembly is trapped between the headstock and tailstock (Photo 14). Lock the tailstock to the bed, release the lock on the quill, and turn the quill knob

to apply light pressure to the glue joint (Photo 15). When the joint is closed all around, set the quill lock. Wipe off the excess glue and allow the assembly to dry overnight.

When the glue has cured, check that everything is still tight and then turn on the lathe (at about 800 RPM). Dress the joint with a square rougher (Photo 16). On most lathes, you won't need to remove the faceplate: it will rotate just fine on the live center. If your lathe doesn't work that way, simply remove the faceplate and snug up the live center.

17 With the base faceplate secured, drill the stepped hole in the top of the orb with a Forstner bit.

18 Leave about ⅛" thickness when drilling. This is a decorative ledge, and is not functional.

In most species, the glue line will virtually disappear. Turn up the speed and sand the entire outside of the assembly, working down through the grits from 80 to 120, 180, 220 and 320. Brush, vacuum or blow away the dust, and then apply several light coats of sprayed, quick-drying gloss lacquer while the piece spins at its slowest speed, being careful not to get any overspray on the bottom face (where the foot will be attached). The idea of applying some finish at this stage is that it will highlight any flaws so they can be fixed before the project is removed from between centers.

When the finish is dry, it's time to drill the opening in the lid for the finial. Fit a standard drill chuck to the tailstock and chuck a 2" Forstner bit in it. The urn should still be attached to the chuck in the headstock. At the lathe's slowest speed, drill the opening (Photo 17), stopping about ³⁄₁₆" shy of the bottom. To check this, retard the bit every now and then and see if the center spur has pierced the wood. As soon as it does, remove the drill chuck and switch to a carbide-tipped detailer. Remove the center of the waste, leaving a small ledge all round (Photo 18). If this process doesn't go well, know that the ledge is just for aesthetic reasons: it has no mechanical function, so you could live without it.

19 Rough turn the foot about ⅛" oversize and then use the lathe as a clamp to glue it in place.

Add the Foot

The foot on this piece begins as a circle that is cut on the band saw from ¹⁰⁄₄ soft maple. Mount it to a faceplate by driving screws into the bottom, and then shape it close to the full-size pattern, leaving it slightly oversized for now (about ⅛"). Unplug the lathe and lay a couple of paper towels on the bed, to catch any excess glue. Then apply glue liberally to the top of the foot and the bottom of the urn. Mount the urn between the foot and the tailstock (Photo 19), placing a jam block between the top of the urn and the tailstock (Photo 20). Apply enough pressure to close the gap and to squeeze out any

20 In order to keep the tailstock safely in place, use a jam block to span the hole in the top.

21 A round carbide tool, used as a scraper, does a great job of cleaning up the glue joint.

excess glue, making sure the parts are centered on each other, and then allow the glue to cure overnight.

When the glue is dry, plug in the lathe and clean up the joint (Photo 21). A round carbide scraper works wonderfully. Then apply several coats of sprayed lacquer to the entire urn as it spins at the lathe's lowest speed, sanding lightly between coats with 400-grit sandpaper. Steel wool tends to leave black residue and even metal fibers behind.

And Finish with the Finial...

For detailed instructions on making finials, see Chapter 9.

The finial here begins life as a length of solid maple, because glued-up stock here will probably reveal a joint line in an awkward spot. Its overall finished length is 9⅞", so the blank needs to be about 12" long. The diameter is 2³⁄₁₆" at the widest point, although you can of course be as creative as you like, and design your own profile.

Mount the finial blank between centers and reduce it to a cylinder using a flat carbide rougher. One could also use a traditional spindle gouge here

22 The maple finial is turned to a cylinder with a square rougher, or a traditional spindle gouge.

(Photo 22), as this is one of a very few situations where a traditional tool is faster than a carbide-tipped one. Following the dimensions in the full-size drawing, turn a tenon on one end (a square rougher at medium speed works well), and then lock the headstock end of the spindle in a chuck. Keep the tailstock in place for now. Use a variety of gouges and scrapers to reveal the desired profile (see Chapter 9) and increase the speed near the end to get cleaner cuts. A spindle rest is handy but not necessary, as the thinnest part of the spire is still a substantial ¼" in diameter. Sharp tools are a must. Leave the tip attached to the waste at the tailstock

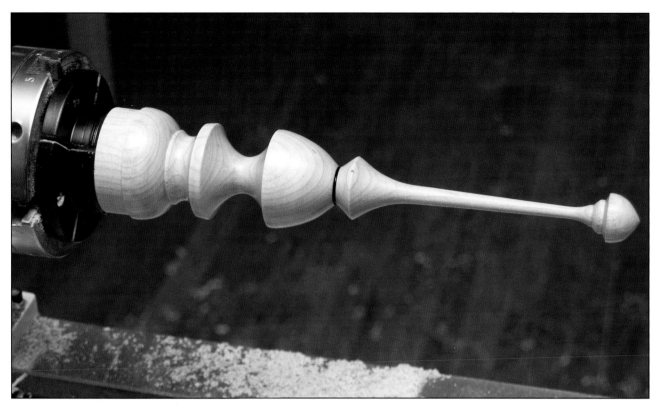

23 Look over Chapter 9 (on making finials) before creating the maple lid for your urn.

end, and just reduce the diameter here to about ⅛". Sand down through the grits (80, 150, 220), and then use a parting tool to sever the tip. Before parting, I used a wire to burn a black ring at the base of the spire (Photo 23), just to add a little flair.

At the plug (the stepped bottom of the finial below the last radius), gently scrape or sand with paper backed by a piece of scrap wood until it fits freely into the top of the urn. This may require removing it several times from the lathe for dry fitting. Mask the plug and spray several coats of lacquer

on the finial, sanding lightly with 400 grit paper between coats. The plug remains unfinished in case somebody wants to glue it in place down the road.

With the urn and finial both completed and finished, turn the urn upside-down to measure the diameter of the base. Cut a circle of felt (available at stationery stores) to about ⅛" smaller than this size, and glue it in place with spray adhesive. Spray only on the felt, to avoid overspray on the urn.

When the glue dries, the project is done.

The Volume of a Sphere

This urn is about the right size for the cremains of a person up to 190 lbs. One pound of body weight requires a little less than one cubic inch. To measure the capacity of any hollow vessel, simply fill it with beans or some other small object, and then decant them into a measuring device. The one shown here (below) has inside dimensions of 4" x 5", so every 1" in height represents 20 cubic inches of volume. The Plexiglas™ front has been scored every inch, to make it easy to read. Beans or beads need to be shaken constantly both in the vessel and in the measuring device, as their volume decreases dramatically as they settle. A funnel is a good idea to prevent spills.

The volume of a sphere is $\frac{4}{3}\pi r^3$.

The beans are probably quicker than the math.

The jig shown uses beans from the grocery story to measure the volume of hollow vessels.

CHAPTER 9

Finials

(Note: A chuck is necessary.)

While bowls, pots and hollow vessels are the most popular turning projects, these forms can be dramatically enhanced by the addition of a finial or a pedestal. Finials are the long spires atop turned works, and pedestals are the legs, or bases. Much as the frame completes a painting, a finial can often turn an ordinary form into something spectacular. Noted turner Sam Angelo from Worland, Wyoming (wyomingwoodturner. com) uses these thin, tapering forms to create Christmas ornaments (following page) and lids for his hollow vessels (following page).

Anna Achtziger, a professional artist who specializes in beaded jewelry, completed the hollow vessel shown here (below, right). A student at the Black Hills School of Woodworking, this was just her third piece ever on a lathe. Not to detract from her innate ability and obvious artistic talent, the incredibly brief learning curve she experienced using carbide insert tools is not terribly unusual. This new generation of tools allows turners to give physical form to their vision quickly and competently, in a way that traditional turning techniques never espoused.

(right, top) A blackwood finial completely changes the character of this crab apple vessel (5" x 8").

(right, bottom) The maple foot and finial on this red oak vessel were made by a novice with carbide cutters.

(below) Finials can be used to make holiday decorations, traditional furniture parts, and lids.

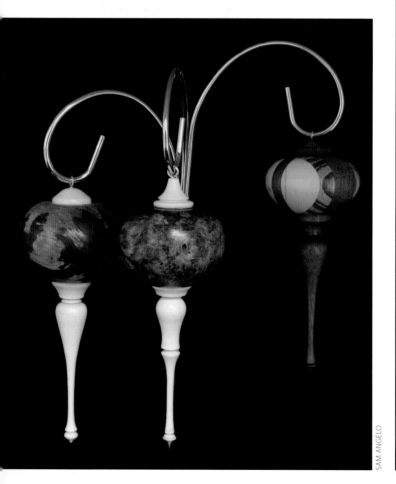

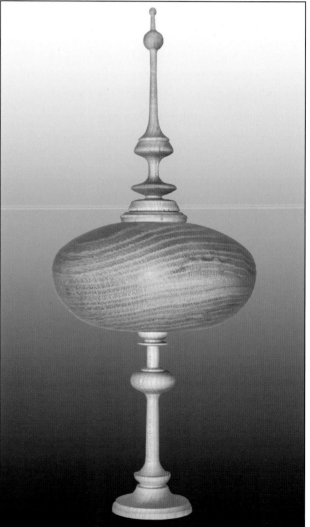

These delicate spires and supports look a lot more challenging to make than they really are. Historically, they have been formed with gouges (which are somewhat aggressive) and scrapers that could often be charged with blunt trauma battery. The new flat-topped carbide cutters cross the line between these tools, delivering a cut that is somewhere between slicing and abrading. As such, they are very easy to control, making it possible to do graceful, fragile and precise work rather quickly.

Project 8: A Maple Finial

Begin by installing a length of square stock in a chuck (Photo 1). The dimensions depend on the capacity of your jaws, but somewhere in the neighborhood of 2" square and perhaps 10" to 12" long will work just fine. This is just a practice piece. Solid lumber is preferable to laminated (glued-up) stock, because glue lines have a tendency to show up in exactly the wrong place in a finished finial (that is, just enough off center to make the piece look unbalanced). However, for practice pieces, glue lines are fine. And hardwoods are better than softwoods, because the latter tend to break more easily.

Draw an X on the un-chucked end of the stock to locate its center, and then bring up the tailstock for support. Align the live center with the middle of the X, and then lock (tighten) the chuck. Set the tool rest and manually rotate the stock to check that nothing is going to hit. Check that the chuck is tight, and then turn on the lathe at about 1000 RPM.

Use a square rougher to reduce the square to a cylinder (Photo 2). Stop about an inch from the chuck to preserve your knuckles. When there are no more flat spots, feel free to reverse the blank so that the round end is in the chuck and the square end is held by the live center in the tailstock, if you

1 Begin by securing a square billet in a chuck. Hickory, maple and similar tight grains work well.

2 Reduce most of the square billet to a cylinder, using a square carbide insert cutter.

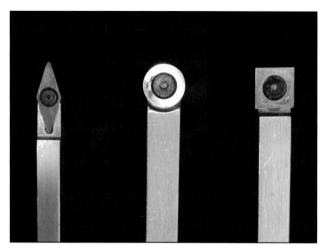

3 Finials are difficult to make unless one has all three carbide insert shapes available.

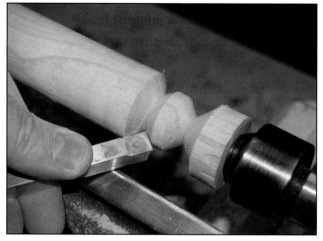

4 Begin the sphere at the top of the finial with two V-cuts made with the square cutter.

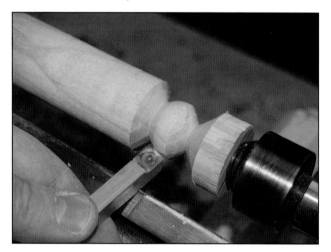

5 Gently sweep the handle of the square tool in a large arc to round over the bottom of the ball.

want a longer finial. Then use the square rougher to complete the cylinder. Note that after reversing the work, it may be a little off center, but one or two light passes along its entire exposed length will correct this.

There are only four shapes on any finial or pedestal. These are outside (convex) curves; inside (concave) curves; grooves (usually V-shaped); and straight runs. All of these can be made with the three basic tools: the square rougher, the round finisher, and the triangular detailer (Photo 3). It's a good idea to invest in two sizes of round finisher, but if the budget only allows for one, opt for a

smaller version. With patience, this tool can cut big curves, but the big tool simply can't fit into very small, tight curves.

One other tool, what professional turners call the "80-grit gouge", is extremely handy when turning finials and delicate, thin objects. It's actually 120, 220 and 320 grit sandpaper.

With the work trued (round), it's time to begin making shapes. The concept here is to begin near the top and complete about ¾" to 1" of the turning at a time. This means that most of your cylinder will remain intact to support the delicate area that is being worked upon. That ¾" needs to be fully formed before the next segment is started, as it simply won't be strong enough to withstand too much impact without this support.

Finials usually terminate in a ball, oval or flame shape. Begin forming this with the tailstock still in place and the lathe turned up to about 1500 RPM (Photo 4). Note that the top of the finial needs to be perhaps ½" in from the end of the cylinder, because the point of the live center has created a small, funnel-shaped hole.

6 Do the same movement in reverse so the cutter can round over the top of the ball.

7 The edges of the pointed detailer clean up the curve, and the top cuts the waste free.

After cutting a couple of V-shapes, turn the bottom one into an outside (convex) curve with a straight cutter (Photo 5). You can practice making various shapes from eggs to round balls, and use the round cutter to make flames that look like skinny Hershey's Kisses™. Shapes can be called domes, coves, mushrooms, umbrellas, plates, tapers and more, but they all boil down to just inside and outside curves.

For now, just make the top of the orb round by swinging the end of the handle in a counterclockwise arc as you travel around the outside curve (Photo 6). Watch the shape emerge at the top of the blank. Place some brown cardboard behind the turning and all its tiny flaws will jump forth. Your last pass should be very gentle. Switch to a detailer to reduce the material at the top of the orb to about $\frac{1}{16}$" in diameter (Photo 7), and then turn off the lathe. Slide the tailstock away, and then snap off the waste (Photo 8). Sand the orb before starting work on the rest of the finial. Medium grits cut more quickly than one would assume, and 180-grit will smooth out the ball in a few seconds. 280-grit will ready it for a finish.

8 Reduce the waste to about $\frac{1}{8}$" diameter, then turn off the lathe and snap off the waste.

The thickness (or more correctly perhaps, the thinness) of the straight runs in a finial or pedestal is related aesthetically to the size of the orb, and functionally to the intended use of the completed piece. If the work is pure art that will be displayed behind glass, the finial can taper thinly away. If the work is a jewelry box that will receive daily handling, the shaft needs to be a lot sturdier (thicker). One of the most startling revelations about turning is that the person who breaks a finial is usually a lot more upset than the one who made it. Perhaps, when we go too thin, we almost expect a mishap.

9 Work down the finial ¾" at a time, allowing the bulk of the blank to support the thin parts.

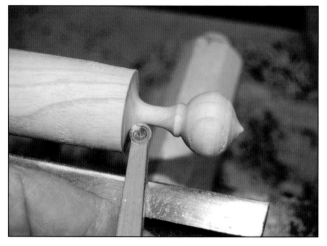

10 Completely finish forming each ¾" segment before moving on to the next one.

11 The concept here is to never have to return to the thin work once each segment is done.

12 Blend the new segment into the old, and sand as you go to avoid stressing the work.

Work down the finial in increments of about ¾" (Photo 9), taking it all the way down to the desired final thickness (Photo 10) before tackling the next ¾" (Photo 11). Note that, once this short length of the shaft has been reduced to its thinnest dimension, it's not okay to go back and clean up with a tool. The work simply can't absorb the shock, so the only way to work on the thin section is with sandpaper. The remaining thick blank will support about twice its own diameter. That is, the 1½" thick piece shown here will allow you to work about 3" of thin spindle without breaking (Photo 12), if you're gentle.

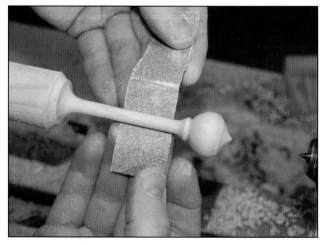

13 Sandpaper, called "the 80-grit gouge" by old turners, is an ideal tool for blending.

14 Squaring off the top of a small detail with a flat cutter is an easy way to remove tearout.

Sand as you go (Photo 13). The farther away from the orb you cut, the weaker the finial becomes, so sand every ¾" section as you finish cutting it.

Bringing two concave cuts together to create a knife-edge is very difficult. The grain will chip out and, no matter how gently you cut, it never seems to create a sharp point without tear-out. One solution is to square off the top of the detail with a rougher (Photo 14), and then lightly sand with very fine paper.

When the thin shaft is long enough, flare it out with the round finisher (Photo 15). Using the intersection of the tool and the tool-rest as a pivot point, cut a smooth sweep in one long, uninterrupted pass (Photo 15). For a more

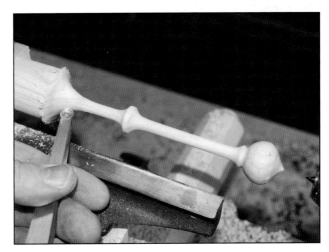

15 Small round cutters work wonderfully on finials for creating sweeping transitions.

decorative transition, switch to the square cutter and create a rabbet (shelf), and an outside curve (Photo 16). Remember that the side of the tool cuts, too. It can be used to smooth out curves on final passes.

16 Rabbets, shallow grooves and outside curves, all cut with a square tool, add texture.

17 The detailer (pointed cutter) is used to define the bottom of the finial, and cut it loose.

18 While parting the finial from the blank, it can be undercut so the edge makes a tight seal.

Begin separating the finial from the waste that is locked in the chuck by cutting a channel with the detailer (Photo 17). It often helps to make the bottom of the part slightly concave, so that there is no gap when it is glued to another part (Photo 18). Sometimes, one can create a small tenon here (Photo 19), and drill a matching hole in the top of a lid or a hollow vessel. For now, let's just separate the parts by reducing the connection to about 1/8" or less in diameter (Photo 20), and then snapping it free with the lathe turned off (Photo 21).

19 Finials can be installed with a small tenon designed to fit in a hole in the top of a lid.

20 Leave some waste on the end of a small blank to keep knuckles away from the chuck.

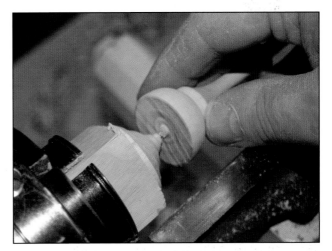

21 Turn off the lathe before snapping small parts loose, and then sand away the small nub.

Species for Making Finials

The best species for making finials are straight, tight-grained woods such as maple, poplar, and sometimes exotics like African blackwood, ebony and teak. Wider grains such as oak, ash and butternut tend to get hairy and even wobble a bit when they get too thin, or they suffer small oblong voids when the tool catches side grain and removes a long splinter.

Wide (coarse) grained woods are more difficult to ebonize, too. This is a process where native species are stained black or black/red to simulate the look of endangered ebony, which has numerous restrictions on its sale and use commercially. Exotic woods often contain oils that exacerbate allergies in many turners, which is a good reason to avoid them and use native US species. Ebonizing can create a striking contrast between a light-colored orb and a black pedestal and finial.

One of the most popular woods for delicate work is African blackwood. According to Bell Forest Products, Inc. of Ishpeming, Michigan, it's "an exotic wood native to Eastern Africa, and is also known as Mozambique Ebony or Senegal Ebony.

It features a dark brown, even purplish heartwood with dark streaks. It is an extremely hard wood, strong and stiff, very stable, with a fine texture. Mainly used for custom pool cues, woodwind instruments, knife handles, walking sticks, and carving. African blackwood is considered one of the world's finest woods

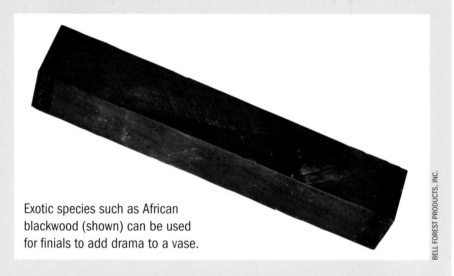

Exotic species such as African blackwood (shown) can be used for finials to add drama to a vase.

BELL FOREST PRODUCTS, INC.

for turning. It polishes very well to a smooth, lustrous finish."

To see some exquisite examples of blackwood finials, visit Colorado woodturner Cindy Drozda's site (cindydrozda.com). Cindy has published a DVD on the subject, titled "Elegant Finials" which has quickly become the industry standard.

CHAPTER 10

The Turning Workshop: Lumber, Lathes, Dust and Safety

Lumber Sources

The vast majority of hobbyist turners use kiln-dried hardwoods for their projects. In part, that's because we have become an urban society, and few of us own chainsaws. For those who do, the lathe can be an artistic instrument. Finding lumber in its natural state opens up a lot of possibilities. There is a good chance of harvesting something special when walking shelterbelts or thinning a woodlot (Photo 1).

Buying hardwoods at an average lumberyard usually restricts turners to ¾" thick boards, but the Internet has changed things. Now, one can do an online search for hardwood sellers across the country, and they will ship thicker blanks right to our doorsteps. However, there is a drawback. Choices have to be made based on photographs or written descriptions, rather than physically seeing and touching the stock. The big advantage of harvesting one's own lumber (or hiring a sawyer to fell a tree for you) is that it can be milled as thick

1 These exquisitely spalted logs were found in a firewood pile in South Dakota's Black Hills.

or thin as you want (Photo 2), and the grain pattern usage can be maximized. Having logs hauled to a small mill, or having a portable mill come to the tree, is surprisingly affordable.

Whether harvesting or buying hardwoods, there are a few things one should know. The first is how hardwoods are measured, and thus sold. There are two units of measurement, thickness and volume. Thickness is counted in "quarters". A rough board that is 1" thick before planning is referred to as 4/4 ("four quarter"). A 1½" thick rough board is 6/4 and a 2" thick slab is 8/4. The industry doesn't add the double hash marks after the number to signify inches.

Volume is counted in board feet. A board foot is 144 cubic inches of rough material. It can be 4" x 6" x 6", or 2" x 3"x 24", or any other combination of three numbers which, when multiplied together, come to 144. This is actually a very simple system. To figure out the price of a turning blank or a board, simply measure its thickness, width and length in inches, multiply them together, divide the result by 144, and then multiply that by the price per board foot. For example, a 12/4 (3") thick slab of walnut that is 9" wide and 72" long contains 13½ board feet of lumber. At, say $7 a BF; the price is

2 Having a small local mill create lumber from your logs can let you make great choices.

$94.50. Sawmills selling rough boards directly to turners and woodworkers will usually round off the numbers in the buyer's favor, to account for wavy natural edges, bark, checking at the ends of the logs and so on (Photo 3). There's room to negotiate.

While a mill may be able to fudge the numbers, a reputable hardwoods lumberyard won't. That's because they're dealing with a processed product. Sawmills usually sell green (still wet) rough lumber, while lumberyards tend to stock kiln-dried boards (Photo 4). Usually, these have been planed just enough to reveal a hint of their grain and color, in a process called "hit and miss". Boards can have a lot of defects, including bow, warp, cup, twist, stain, cracks, checks, knots, insect damage, wane, mill marks and mineral streaks (Photo 5).

3 Small sawmills will generally make allowances for board feet that are bark, splits, etc.

4 Mills sell green (wet) or air-dried boards, as opposed to lumberyards' kiln dried stock.

Hardwoods are most often sold in random widths and lengths. The boards in a specific bundle (called a "bunk") will all be of the same nominal thickness, such as 4/4 or 8/4. They will be of varying ("random") widths, which can be anywhere from 2" to 20" or more, depending on the species. Poplar boards, for example are often close to two feet wide, while quartersawn white oak will usually be in the 4" to 8" wide range.

Random lengths usually run from 3' to 16'. Whenever lengths are specified (that is, when a buyer says that he/she wants specific lengths), the price goes up. As with widths, it is less expensive to specify a range (say, 8' to 12'), than to demand specific lengths (all 10'). However, there are times when specific widths actually save money. For example, if a turner is going to glue up lots of 4" square blanks, he/she won't want to buy a lot of six and seven inch wide stock, because of the amount of waste (drop).

Hardwood boards are often two or three inches longer than the nominal length. For example, an eight-footer may be 99" long. This is because the logs go into the kiln at that length, and unlike softwoods, the ends are not usually trimmed before

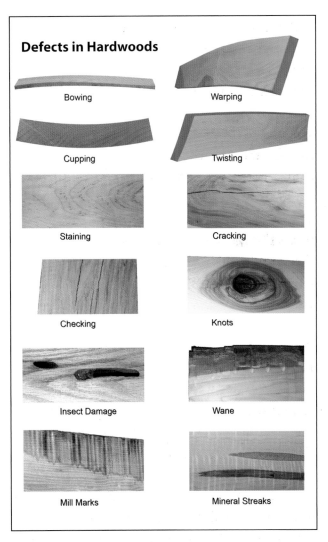

Defects in Hardwoods

Bowing

Warping

Cupping

Twisting

Staining

Cracking

Checking

Knots

Insect Damage

Wane

Mill Marks

Mineral Streaks

5 There are myriad defects in hardwoods, but not all of them make the lumber useless.

sale. When calculating the board feet to charge, most yards will include those three inches, as long as the end isn't split or otherwise damaged.

When figuring out how much lumber to buy, keep in mind that narrow strips can often be edge-glued to make wider boards, but it's virtually impossible to turn short boards into long ones. There are a few router bits that create end joints (Photo 6), but the results usually aren't very pleasing to the eye, especially when turned.

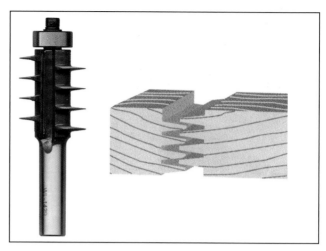

6 Beyond this router bit, there are few tools that can make decent end-to end joints.

Kiln and Air Dried Lumber

All wood contains some moisture. When buying hardwoods, it pays to know a little about moisture levels. The industry measures this in terms of the weight of the water expressed as a percentage of the weight of the wood. For example, imagine an oak board that weighs 42 lbs. without any water in it at all. That same board in a lumberyard in the middle of the country will have a moisture level of about 6% after it has been kiln dried (humidity varies with location and time of year: think Seattle and Death Valley). At 6%, there will be 2.52 lbs. of water in the board, for a total of 44.52 lbs. The water weighs six percent of the net total that the lumber weighs.

This number is important to wholesalers who transport lumber, because fresh logs can have upwards of 30% moisture levels, which means that the trucker can only load about ⅔ of the weight he could legally carry if the load was completely dry.

This number is also important to the turner, because lumber above about 9% tends to misbehave. It splits near the ends, warps, bends and generally has a mind of its own. The moisture isn't evenly distributed (the center of a board is generally wetter than the surfaces), and this can play havoc with the wood when the water expands

7 Jim Birkemeier of Timbergreen Farms in Wisconsin sells plans to build solar wood kilns.

8 This myrtlewood bowl blank was rough turned and then kiln dried in southern Oregon.

9 One never knows what's hiding inside a rough blank until the initial turning is done.

as it heats up during the day, and then contracts as it cools at night.

For their own comfort, people like to control the indoor ambient humidity (the amount of water in the air in a room). We like our air to be around 30% to 50% relative humidity, and fortunately lumber likes the same range. Relative humidity below 20% and above 75% can cause problems with wood. Turners who keep dried hardwoods stored inside are much better off than those who buy from mills and yards that store them outdoors.

Lumber is dried in two ways. It is kiln dried (in a solar, gas, wood or electric oven), or it is seasoned (Photo 7). Seasoning means that the lumber is stickered outdoors, usually under a shed roof or some plastic, and allowed to air dry. Typically, seasoning takes about one year for every inch of thickness, while the average kiln run is just

twenty to forty days, depending on species, kiln size, moisture content and thickness. Stickering means that boards are stacked with ¼" thick sticks between them, to allow air to flow around all six surfaces. If the sticks are not of the same species as the boards, they can leave shadow marks every few feet across the boards, where chemicals in the two species react with each other, and this is something to be aware of and look for when selecting boards.

Turners who harvest their own lumber generally crosscut it into viable blanks (a little longer than they are wide), and then wrap it in plastic until they're ready for a first turning. This "green" turning brings a bowl down to roughly its final shape, although the walls are left quite thick (over an inch) (Photo 8). Then, the blank is waxed and stored for a year per inch of thickness, after which it is put back on the lathe and finish turned to its final shape (Photo 9).

Color and Grain

Boards of the same species can diversify widely when it comes to overall color and general appearance. For example, oak growing in northern Minnesota has a much shorter growing season than oak grown in the southern Appalachians, so it has tighter annual rings. The minerals in the soil, the angle and intensity of the sun, rainfall levels, pollution in the air, and quality of the groundwater all affect the way a tree grows, and the color of its heartwood. Whether or not the tree has neighbors can play a big role. A tree growing alone in a field spreads out to catch as many rays as it can, while one living in a forest needs to grow straight and tall so that it can poke its head out above its neighbors to get a tan. Hardwoods are by nature dendritic, which means they divide into branches and then twigs (Photo 10). (The term is also used to describe the way cells divide and crystals grow.) Curtailing this tendency by planting trees close together is one way to make them grow straight, a deliberate practice that is often associated with mahogany and teak farms in tropical climates. Lumber for turning must be harvested from vertical growth. A horizontal branch (one growing straight out from the trunk of the tree) has different stresses at the top of it than it does at the bottom, and these reveal themselves as cracks and deformities in bowls and vessels.

NHLA Hardwood Lumber Grades

Lumberyards and even sawmills will charge different prices for different grades of lumber, although it's a mystery how a mill can know what grade the wood is inside a log when all they can see is the butt (Photo 11). Grading is theoretically a very precise practice that could be replicated anywhere on the continent. In practice, small mills and even some retailers have their own systems (and terminology) that can be very confusing. The following grades have been developed by the

10 Hardwoods are dendritic, which means they divide into branches and then twigs.

In America, northern hardwoods tend to have more even color from tree to tree than those growing in the South, or across the Appalachians. There also is less of a contrast between the sapwood and heartwood within each tree. Therefore, slow growing northern hardwoods tend to fetch a better price than logs from other parts of the country, but they don't always deliver as dramatic a turning. So, it's a good practice to ask a supplier where his stock originated.

11 How can a mill know what grade the wood is inside a log, when all they can see is the butt?

National Hardwood Lumber Association (NHLA), and have been adopted by most industry groups and producers across the country.

FAS/1F (Firsts and Seconds/ #1 Furniture): 6" and wider, 8' and longer, 83.3% clear on its best face.

Select: 4" and wider, 6' and longer, 83.3% clear on its best face.

#1 Common: 3" and wider, 4' and longer, 66.6% clear on its worst face.

#2A Common: 3" and wider, 4' and longer, 50.0% clear on its worst face.

#2B Common: 3" and wider, 4' and longer, 50.0% sound on its worst face.

#3A Common: 3" and wider, 4' and longer, 33.3% clear on its worst face.

#3B Common: 3" and wider, 4' and longer, 25.0% clear on its worst face.

A buyer should be aware that these basic grading requirements are often relaxed a bit when it comes to less widely available species such as black walnut. And turners generally prefer wood with defects, as long as they are stable enough to turn safely.

Color grades are quite subjective and can change from mill to mill. For example, #1 and #2 White, and the term "Saps" are all grades for maple and birch that describe the amount of sapwood present. Some species are more valued for sap than heartwood, but oak, cherry, walnut, hickory and birch are more valued for brown (heart) color.

Choosing a Lathe

This can be a challenging choice, because there is such a huge variety available. There are small pen lathes that fit on a corner of a workbench, or mini and midi lathes that cover most hobby requirements, and dedicated bowl lathes that are designed with the professional turner in mind. Budget plays a role in the decision, as does available space and, most importantly, the type of work one wants to do.

Mini and Midi Lathes

Because of the eccentric nature of blanks (almost all lathe work begins with a piece of wood that is off-center), lathes need to be able to resist or absorb vibration. They do that in two ways: they are either so heavy that their sheer mass absorbs the motion, or they are secured to walls and/or the floor in such a way as to be able to use the building's mass. If the workshop is up a flight of stairs where hauling a huge machine is a problem, then the second option is usually preferable. Even then, the heaviest lathe possible is most likely the best choice. Lathe stands can help. If a shelf is available, sandbags on a stand can add a lot of stability to a smaller lathe.

A good way to start choosing a lathe is to work backwards. What exactly will it be used for ? If the primary interest is pens, bottle stoppers, ball and cup games and other small projects, then the search can be narrowed to mini lathes. Generally, this category covers machines that have a 10" or less swing. That is, the distance from the center of the drive shaft to the ways (the bed) is no more than 5". The biggest bowl diameter on such a lathe is reasonably about 9", as the blank will need to be trued (made perfectly round). That means the finished project will be smaller than the original work-piece. And it's probably a good idea to plan a little smaller than that. Blanks no bigger than about 75% of full capacity are perhaps a wiser choice, especially when working with irregularly shaped green wood or very dense material.

Midi lathes cover the ground well for most turners, as they will handle bowls up to about 12" in diameter, and sometimes more. They are fairly affordable (most lie in the range of $500 to $1,500), heavy enough to work on, and yet light enough to maneuver into the shop. Things to consider are the amount of power they deliver (more is obviously better), their universality (a 1"-8 thread is the most popular configuration for chucks and other aftermarket options), and the length of the bed. While most beds can be extended to accommodate long stock, some models don't offer this option for turning between centers (spindle turning). The size of the post on the tool rest is a consideration: changing from the stock, short, straight rest to a curved one, or installing a vessel hollowing system can be problematic. It may require that the receiver (the hole) in the banjo (the base of the tool rest) is different than the one offered by the factory. Before buying the lathe, it's a good idea to check out the requirements for these options.

12 Electronic variable speed (EVS), with a dial that displays RPM, is handy but not essential.

Midi lathes are an excellent choice for hobbyists who make small to medium-sized bowls and hollow vessels, or spindles and stair/deck parts. They can be used for pen-making, minor duplicating, faceplate and chuck work, and most come with a speed range of five or six incremental rotations from 500 to 3000 RPM.

Electronic variable speed is an option on many lathes. Changing speeds manually with belts only takes a few seconds with practice, so the rheostat (speed dialing option) is perhaps a luxury rather than a necessity (Photo 12). It's akin to driving a vehicle with an automatic transmission instead of a manual: you still arrive on time. While there are obviously instances where it would be convenient, EVS does command a significant price—about the cost of a couple of top-of-the-line carbide insert tools. And those carbide cutters seem to require a lot fewer speed changes than traditional tools.

Full-Size Lathes

Every new turner dreams of owning a full-size machine with its solid mass, excess power, smooth operation, and a host of built-in options that are standard fare on these biggest of toys. The investment is significant: they run anywhere from the cost of a simple divorce to the kind of money that gets mentioned in a pre-nup, and they're physically large enough that a spouse will definitely notice one in the garage.

Full-size lathes (usually 16" swing and above) are most often defined as such because they are floor models with an integrated stand, rather than bench-top lathes. Many have single features that alone make them worth the investment, such as a power head that slides along the ways so that it can be used at the end of the lathe for outboard turning on very large diameter work. The speed range generally goes from zero to about 3500 RPM or more, the spindle is usually more than 1" in diameter, the motor is 1½ HP or above, and the machine can weigh anything from 500 to 2000 lbs.

Dedicated Bowl Lathes

Mini, midi and full-size lathes are widely available and reviews are very easy to find online. The same is not true for dedicated bowl lathes, so they warrant a little discussion. While the standard, familiar lathe configuration is ideal for spindle turning between centers, serious bowl turners have long objected to it because they can't stand directly in front of the work, as the bed is always in the way.

Several companies have listened to bowl turners and have designed lathes that are heavier, more ergonomical, and much easier to use when turning bowls than the traditional long-bed models. Vega Enterprises Inc., located in Decatur, Illinois, offers two lathes that are specifically designed for bowl turning and both are made in the USA. The smaller machine, the 2413B, is a benchtop model that is relatively affordable for serious turners. It can handle work up to 24" in diameter, and the reversing motor allows sanding in both directions for a very smooth finish. Speeds run from 200 RPM to 2900 RPM, and the 2413B comes with a 1¼" diameter 8 TPI (threads per inch) spindle.

RACHEL SCHEFFEL, WOODS OF WISDOM

13 Some lathes are designed for bowl making, like the Vega owned by master turner Will Bellucci.

Vega's larger Model 2600 bowl lathe has a full 24" swing over the bed and it comes with a removable tailstock that is used to start large work at slow speed (Photo 13). This is a serious machine for serious turners. Made of fabricated steel with

14 VB36 North American rep Greg Jensen turns a massive ash bowl on his British lathe.

concrete ballast in the headstock, users almost universally claim that it is completely vibration-free. There's a manual variable speed 1½ HP motor (115V or 220V with speeds of 800 to 2200 RPM), or a 2 HP (220V) electronic variable speed ranging from 0 to 2520 RPM. Both motors are reversing, and the 2600 has a 1¼" x 8 TPI spindle that adjusts from 37" to 45" to suit turners of varying stature. It weighs 500 lbs. and features a removable steel mesh guard. For more information, visit Vega online at www.vegawoodworking.com.

The VB36 Master Bowlturner Lathe, a British machine, is available through Craft Supplies at woodturnerscatalog.com. Standard capacities are 36" diameter and 30" between centers, but larger projects up to an incredible 92" in diameter can be turned using the company's optional freestanding tool-rest. The VB36 uses high-end "plain" bearings on its shaft. Controls are mounted in a magnetic box that can be stuck on any flat metal surface, for left or right-handed users. They include a reverse switch and variable speed. The lathe is set up for optional footswitch controls, which are handy when tackling some maneuvers such as deep hollowing. The VB36 comes with a 2HP 3-phase motor wired through a phase converter, so it uses standard 240-voltage. Speed ranges are from

50 to 2600 RPM. It weighs from 583 lbs. to 689 lbs., depending on its configuration. VB's freestanding tool-rest (optional) can be placed anywhere around the work, allowing a turner to concentrate on the back and outer rim of a large diameter work-piece (Photo 14). Outrigger legs are available to extend its footprint for stability. The rest, called a VB80, can also be positioned behind or alongside the turner to act as a support for long, handled deep hollowing tools. In this mode, two rests effectively control the tool.

Dust Collection on the Lathe

Aside from a radial arm or miter saw, no piece of woodshop equipment is as difficult to set up for dust collection as a lathe. Various suppliers offer different plastic hoods that are designed to collect chips as they are generated, but because turners are constantly moving and attacking the work from different angles, these solutions are often more annoying than helpful.

The assumption is that dust collection is necessary, and it is. But, is chip collection necessary? Most of the waste generated by carbide cutters is heavy dust or small chips. The fine dust doesn't really come into play until one begins to sand on the lathe. Visible dust particles are actually so large that most medical experts are not too concerned about them. It's sub-micron dust that plays havoc with our respiratory systems. Sure, large dust particles need to be cleaned up before they become a slipping hazard on the floor, but turners who have been exasperated by trying to collect all their lathe chips, and who have given up on dust collection, might want to consider this. It's fairly easy to hold a dust collection hose in one hand, and sandpaper in the other. Collecting the fines before they become airborne will eliminate most of the dust-related hazards associated with woodturning.

Don't sand without a shop vacuum or dust collector running.

Woodturner's Blast Gates

Lathes create lots of small chips, and both plastic and aluminum gates have small channels in them that routinely become clogged with these. The simple blast gate shown here eliminates channels. It's just a plate dropped into a slot. Having only two parts, it's easy to make and involves building three very simple jigs. After that, each gate costs less than a dollar to make. The process also uses up all of the short scrap left over when plastic ductwork is installed.

Step 1: Cut 4" diameter PVC pipe into 7" lengths (one for each gate). This can be done on a miter saw, but the safest way is to build a plywood sled (Photo 1) with runners attached to the bottom to guide it against the sides of the band saw table. A stop attached to the back edge stops the cut when the blade is halfway through the back fence.

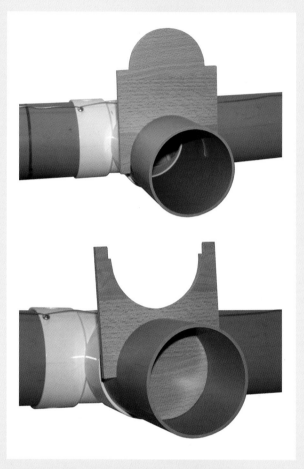

Lathes can clog up blast gates, but not these shop-made ones with no gate grooves.

1 The safest way to cross-cut plastic pipe to make your own gates is on the band saw.

Step 2: Locate the slot (Photo 2). This requires drawing two pencil lines on the outside of the pipe, parallel to each other and 180° apart (that is, opposite each other). Make a three-part cradle with walls half as tall as the diameter of the pipe, drop the pipe in place and draw the lines (Photo 3).

Step 3: Install a ⁵⁄₁₆" plunge bit in the router table and adjust the height of the exposed bit to roughly ¹⁄₁₆" taller than the thickness of the plastic pipe. It just has to peek through. Lock the fence so that the center of the bit is 2⅛" (half the OD of the pipe) in front of it.

Step 4: Make a one-piece, C-shaped guide on the band saw (Photo 4), and attach it to the fence with clamps.

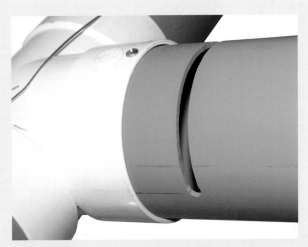

2 The gates simply drop into a slot that is milled in the pipe with a plunge router bit.

3 Build a simple jig to locate the centerline halfway up each side of a piece of pipe.

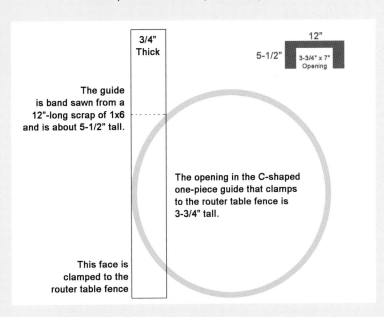

4 An auxiliary fence on the router table has a gap the length of the pipe, to stop it wandering.

The guide is band sawn from a 12"-long scrap of 1x6 and is about 5-1/2" tall.

3/4" Thick

This face is clamped to the router table fence

12"
5-1/2" 3-3/4" x 7" Opening

The opening in the C-shaped one-piece guide that clamps to the router table fence is 3-3/4" tall.

5 The cut for the slot begins with one of the centerlines lined up on the edge of the fence.

6 The cut will stop when the second pencil line is rolled forward until it reaches the fence.

Step 5: Turn on the router and slowly lower the pipe into the guide so that one of the pencil marks lines up with the front edge of the guide (Photo 5).

Step 6: Rotate the top of the pipe (keeping your fingers close to the ends) toward the fence, and stop when the second pencil mark lines up with the front edge of the guide (Photo 6). Turn off the machine, and when the bit stops revolving, remove the pipe.

Step 7: To make the matching gate (Photo 7), mark the outline on a laminate flooring remnant (Photo 8) (installers have lots of free, short

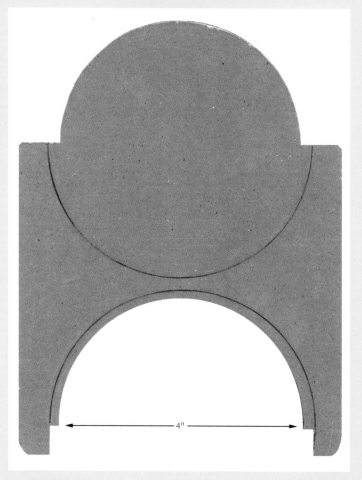

7 Each gate, made from scrap laminate flooring, has an open and a closed end.

leftovers), and then cut it out on the band saw (Photo 9). Clean up the edges with a file and a drum sander (Photo 10). These gates work best when installed anywhere between 5° and 90° to the floor, so that gravity helps them stay in place when the airflow stops. Slide them into the slot in one direction for open, and in the other for closed. The slot in the pipe is always "up", so there's nowhere for turning chips to accumulate.

8 Once the first gate is made, it can be used as a template to lay out as may as you need.

9 Cut each gate carefully on the band saw to minimize the amount of sanding required.

10 Clean up the inside curves on a drum sander, and the outside corners with a fine file.

Lathe Safety

Working with any power tool can be hazardous. The following is not an exhaustive list of safety topics, but it covers most of the dangers. As with any power tool, we must use common sense and remember that if it feels unsafe, it probably is.

One should never wear loose clothing or jewelry when working on a lathe. Short sleeves are strongly advised, as is a turning smock.

Long hair (including a long beard) must be tied back, or at some point it's pretty much guaranteed that it will become embroiled in the lathe. We tend to lean forward to get a better look, and it only takes a second....

Open-toed shoes are an accident waiting to happen. Heavy things (chucks, blanks) tend to drop. And sharp tools nearly always head for the turf point first.

Safety glasses are a minimum requirement, but most of the inexpensive ones seem to distort one's vision, so a plastic face shield ($15-$25 at hardware stores) is a sound investment and offers far more protection.

Most turning produces fairly heavy particles that are more apt to hurt a person by impact (flying through the air) than by being inhaled. However, sanding on the lathe produces a lot of fine particles, and should only be done when a dust collector or vacuum is in use. Don't use a shop vacuum or dust collector when spraying volatile finishes, as the residue may ignite or even explode.

Earplugs are a good idea if one is running a shop vacuum, but most lathe work is not a threat to one's hearing (it's under 60 decibels) and being able to hear a rattle is important.

Sweep the floor regularly. Fine dust can be as slippery as ice, especially on a varnished hardwood or laminate floor.

When chucking or mounting a piece of wood between centers, check it all the way around and on the ends for cracks or splits. If there's a crack, go ahead and split it, and then use the segments for smaller, safer projects.

Provide plenty of light that can be focused directly on the work. Seeing a crack before it becomes a problem can save both the work piece and the worker.

Shut off the lathe before physically touching or inspecting work. Let it come to a complete stop before reaching toward it.

After turning off the lathe, never grab the wheel at the outside of the headstock to slow down or stop a lathe that has a chuck or a faceplate installed. This can cause the chuck or plate to unthread itself, and it happens in the blink of an eye. It will go airborne.

Everything needs to be tight, including the tool rest, the banjo and the tailstock. Check twice before turning on the power.

Don't stand in the line of fire when the lathe starts up. Something may fly! And if it rattles, **turn it off**.

On mini and midi lathes, it's perhaps best to stay within 75% or so of the capacity when the work is off center. For example, don't mount a natural log larger than about nine inches on a twelve-inch lathe.

Use sturdy dome-head screws (rather than brittle sheetrock screws) to mount work to a faceplate, and drive the screws into pre-drilled pilot holes to avoid cracking the wood. Faceplates with more than four screws are safer.

Start at the slowest speed, especially with work that isn't yet round. If the lathe shakes, shut off the power and revisit the band saw.

Use the tailstock whenever possible. Period.

Keep First Aid supplies handy.

Let someone know when you're going to be alone in the shop.

Small grandchildren need to go home now.

Sources

Carbide Wood Turning Tools

carbidewoodturningtools.com	info@carbidewoodturningtools.com	N/A

Easy Wood Tools, USA

1. easywoodtools.com	service@easywoodtools.com	859-246-0294
2. BHSW Inc.	bhsw.org	605-591-2947
3. David J. Marks	djmarks.com	N/A
4. King Arthur Tools	katools.com	800-942-1300
5. Highland Woodworking	highlandwoodworking.com	800-241-6748
6. CU Woodshop Supply	cuwoodshop.com	217-355-1244
7. Woodworkers Shop	woodworkersshop.com	800-475-9663
8. WoodTurningz	woodturningz.com	888-736-5487
9. Bargain Supply Company	bargainsupply.com	800-322-5226
10. Choice Woods	choice-woods.com	888-895-7779
11. Manny's Woodworkers Place	store.mannyswoodworkersplace.com	800-243-0713
12. Kenyon Noble Lumber	kenyonnoble.com	406-586-2384
13. The Woodworking Source	the-woodworking-source.com	775-624-9174
14. Cason Builder Supply	casonbuildersupply.com	800-242-9222
15. Woodcraft Stores	woodcraft.com	800-225-1153
16. Klingspor Woodworking Shops	woodworkingshop.com	800-228-0000

17. Packard Woodworks	packardwoodworks.com	800-683-8876
18. Woodworking Source	thewoodworkingsource.com	704-658-1111
19. EB Mueller	muellerco.com	800-642-5656
20. Hartville Tool	hartvilletool.com	330-877-4685
21. Wood Werks Supply	woodwerks.com	800-860-9375
22. Mann Tool and Supply, Inc.	manntools.com	803-252-7777
23. WoodZone	woodzone.com	803-791-3823
24. Woodwork Shop, Inc.	thewoodworkshopinc.com	901-755-355
25. Wood World of Texas	woodworldtx.com	972-669-9130
26. Craft Supplies USA	woodturnerscatalog.com	800-551-8876
27. A-Line Machine Tool	alinetools.com	606-785-1515
28. Heartland Hardwoods	heartlandhardwoods.com	715-834-7792
29. Withrow's Woodworking	withrowsales.com	304-736-7262

Easy Wood Tools, Worldwide

1. Austria	Neureiter - Maschinen und Werkzeuge	drechselmaschinen.at	N/A
2. Canada	Lee Valley & Veritas	leevalley.com	800-267-8767
3. Canada	Woodchucker's Supplies	woodchuckers.com	800-551-0192
4. Japan	Mokko-senban-dokokai	woodturning@qc.commufa.jp	053 437 1219
5. New Zealand	Steel Toolz Ltd.	steelgi@hotmail.com	021 103 8844
6. Norway	Gustavsen AS	gustavsenas.no	47 99 58 01 20

| 7. South Korea | John Kim's Craft Art Co. | jongjkkim@yahoo.com | 82 (0)31-913-0248 |
| 8. United Kingdom | Wood Workers Workshop | woodworkersworkshop.co.uk | 44 (0)1491 629699 |

Harrison Specialties

| harrisonspecialties.com | kerry@harrisonspecialties.com | 763-441-0176 |

Hunter Tool Systems

1. hunterwoodturningtool.com	mike@hunterwoodturningtool.com	612-718-7926
2. Turning Wood	turningwood.com	972-424-7958
3. Woodcraft Stores	woodcraft.com	800-225-1153
4. Craft Supplies USA	woodturnerscatalog.com	800-551-8876
5. Packard Woodworks, Inc.	packardwoodworks.com	800-683-8876
6. Woodchuckers's Supplies	woodchuckers.com	800-551-0192
7. VERKTØY AS, Norway	verktoyas.no	+47 51 88 68 00

J&B Tools

| jandbtools.com | cutoff1@aol.com | 251-510-7805 |

Jewelwood Studios/Eliminator

| 1. Craft Supplies USA | woodturnerscatalog.com | 800-551-8876 |
| 2. Packard Woodworks, Inc. | packardwoodworks.com | 800-683-8876 |

Mike Jackofsky's Hollow-Pro Tools

Craft Supplies USA woodturnerscatalog.com 800-551-8876

New Edge Cutting Tools

newedgecuttingtools.com newedgetools@aol.com 860-628-4642

Rockler Woodworking and Hardware

rockler.com orders@rockler.com 800-279-4441

Unique Tool/Things Western

thingswestern.com uniquetl@vtc.net 800-840-2434

Wood-of-1-Kind

wood-of-1-kind.webs.com pcribari@hotmail.com N/A

Munro Hollowing Tools

Craft Supplies USA woodturnerscatalog.com 800-551-8876

Index

A-Line Machine Tool 123

AAW 1

"Achtziger, Anna" 96

African Blackwood 104

All in One Wood Tools 73

American Association of Woodturners 1

"Angelo, Sam" 95

Bargain Supply Company 122

"Bellucci, Will" 113

Between centers 43, 73

Blackhawk Tools 30

"Blast gate, shop-built" 116

Board feet 106

Boss Hogger 27

Bowl 63, 64, 66

Carbi-Universal 30

Carbide 5, 7

Carbide Depot 30

Carbide Wood Turning Tools 15, 32, 122

Carbon 5

Cason Builder Supply 122

"Castelin, Eddie" 30

Choice Woods 122

Choosing a lathe 111

Choosing tools 12

Chuck 53

Ci1 square Rougher 44

Clean-up pass 37

Color and grain 110

Compound hollow vessel 85

Cost 11

Craft Supplies USA 25, 29, 34, 114, 123, 124, 125

"Cribari, Peter" 28, 31, 38

Crossgrain hollow vase 71

CU Woodshop Supply 122

Cutter shape 10, 33

Defects in lumber 107

Dendritic trend 110

Detailer 18, 46, 48, 55, 102

Difficult grain 38

Digger 22

Drilling on a lathe 91

"Drozda, Cindy" 104

Dull 12

Dust collection 115

East Texas Woodturners' Association 83

Easy Hollower 69, 72, 73

Easy Wood Tools (EWT) 10, 18, 19, 32, 37, 38, 39, 44, 69, 122

EB Meuller 123

Eliminator 23, 42

Faceplate 19, 49, 59, 89

Finial 92, 95, 104

Finisher 18, 46, 48, 50, 54

Finishing 81, 88

Gluing: Use lathe as a clamp 90

Grading 110

Green lumber 109

Gustavsen AS 123

Harrison Specialties 20, 32, 124,

"Harrison, Kerry" 20

Hartville Tool 123

Heartland Hardwoods 123

Hercules 67

Highland Woodworking 122

"Holder, Fred" 41

Hollow Pro Tools 24, 32, 38, 39, 125

Hollow vessel 69

Hollower 18

Hunter Tool Systems 14, 21, 32, 40, 41, 64, 65, 66, 67, 81, 82, 124

"Hunter, Mike" 21, 40

"Insert, concave" 63

"Insert, flat-topped" 34, 51

"Insert, square" 35

J&B Tools 22, 32, 124

"Jackofsky, Mike" 24, 32, 38, 39, 40, 125

"Jackson, Craig" 10, 37

Jam block 58, 87

Jaws 53, 55, 68, 83

"Jensen, Greg" 114

JET 87

Jewelwood Studios 23, 32, 124

John Kim's Craft Art Co. 124

Kenyon Noble Lumber 122

Kiln and air-dried lumber 108

King Arthur Tools 122

Klingspor Woodworking Shops 122

Knob 60

Lathe safety 120

Lathe speed 34, 44

Lathe: bowl 113

Lathe: full-size 113

Lathe: midi 112

Lathe: mini 111

Lee Valley & Veritas 123

Live center 43, 58, 76

"Lucas, John" 41

Lumber sources 105

Machinery's Handbook 9

"Mann Tool and Supply, Inc." 123

Manny's Woodworkers Place 122

"Marks, David J." 4, 122

"McDaniel, Jack" 23, 42

"McNight, Bill" 30
Mokko-senban-dokokai 123
More Woodturning 41
Mozambique Ebony 104
Munro Tools Ltd. 29, 32, 125
Myrtlewood 109
Nano-carbide 5
Neureiter - Maschinen und
    Werkzeuge 123
New edge Cutting Tools 25, 32, 125
NHLA hardwood grades 110
"Nish, Dale" 34
Oneway Manufacturing 73
Packard Woodworks 29, 123, 124
Peeler 22
Project: Basic bowl - Concave
    Cutter 63
Project: Basic bowl - Flat Cutter, 51
Project: Hickory Candlestick 43
Project: Lidded Bowl 56
Project: Long Grain Hollow Vase 74
Project: Oak Vase 69
Project: Undercut Pot 63
Project: Urn 85
Random length 107
Random width 107
Rockler Woodworking and Hardware
    26, 32, 125
"Rollings, Joe and Janet" 27
Rotondo 28
Rougher 18, 46, 47, 50
Safety 120
Sanding 55, 80, 87
Sawmill 106
"Scheffel, Rachel" 32
Senegal Ebony 104

Shaft shape 13, 34
"Shaft, flat round" 42
"Shaft, round" 40
"Shaft, square" 34
Shaver 22
Shield 19
Skogger 28
Solar kiln 108
Species for finials 104
Spur drive 43
"St. Leger, Mark" 82
Steady rest 73
Steel Toolz Ltd. 123
Swan neck 39, 72
Tenon 53, 56, 57, 83
The Woodworking Source 122
Tool Brace 17
Tool handles 13
Tool rest 35, 55
Tool rest height 35, 36
"Tool rest, using two rests" 42, 72
Tungsten carbide 5, 6
Turning between centers 43, 73
Turning Wood 124
Unique Tools/Things Western 27, 32,
    125
Variable speed 112
VB36 Bowlturner 114
Vega 113
"VERKTØY AS, Norway" 124
Volume of a hollow vessel 94
"Walz, Tom" 8
Waxed blank 109
Withrow's Woodworking 123
Wolframite 5
Wood Werks Supply 123

Wood Workers Workshop 124
Wood World of Texas 123
Wood-of-1-Kind 28, 32, 38, 125
Woodchucker's Supplies 123, 124
Woodcraft Stores 122, 124
WoodTurningz 122
"Woodwork Shop, Inc." 123
Woodworkers Shop 122
Woodworking Source 123
WoodZone 2, 123

About the Author

John English has been building furniture and cabinets for more than thirty years. His woodshop writing and photography has appeared in about thirty books and over a thousand magazine articles. His wife, Dr. Meg English, is his favorite editor. John teaches furniture design/building and woodturning at the Black Hills School of Woodworking (bhsw.org) in Belle Fourche, South Dakota.